Marriage and Divorce Law in South Carolina

Fourth Edition

A Layperson's Guide

by
Roy T. Stuckey

The South Carolina Bar and its Continuing Legal Education Division do not render any legal, accounting, or other professional services. South Carolina Bar - Continuing Legal Education publications are intended to provide current and accurate information about the subject matter covered, and are designed to help attorneys maintain their professional competence. Attorneys using South Carolina Bar - Continuing Legal Education publications in dealing with a specific client's or their own legal matters should also research original sources of authority.

The author has obtained information from sources believed to be reliable. However, because of human or mechanical error, neither the author nor the South Carolina Bar guarantees the accuracy, adequacy or completeness of any information or forms and is not responsible for errors or omissions or for the results obtained from use of such information and/or forms contained in this book.

The South Carolina Bar - Continuing Legal Education Division would appreciate any comments or notification of any errors. Such comments may be forwarded, in writing please, to:

The South Carolina Bar
Continuing Legal Education Division
Attention: Publications Director
Post Office Box 608
Columbia, South Carolina
29202-0608

About the Author
and the Board of Editors

Roy T. Stuckey was a professor of law at the University of South Carolina School of Law for over 34 years. He taught family law as well as professional skills and clinical courses. He is the author of MARITAL LITIGATION IN SOUTH CAROLINA: SUBSTANTIVE LAW, 4th Ed. (SC Bar - CLE Division 2010), which is recognized as the primary legal resource for divorce lawyers and Family Court judges in South Carolina. Professor Stuckey was born and raised in Sumter. He is a graduate of Davidson College (1970) and the University of South Carolina School of Law (1973). Although Professor Stuckey is a member of the South Carolina Bar, he does not accept private clients. He was ably assisted in the preparation of this book by several law students: Amy Haines, Hayes Walsh, and Heather Shirley (first edition), Camey Everhart (second edition), Miranda Dynes (third edition), and Meagan Diedolf (fourth edition).

The first edition of the book was reviewed by a board of editors consisting of lawyers and nonlawyers. At least one lawyer from each of the sixteen judicial circuits in South Carolina was invited to serve on the board of editors, and lawyers from ten judicial circuits actually participated in the editing process. The lawyers who reviewed initial drafts of the book collectively provide legal representation to all types of people in all categories of divorce litigation around South Carolina. Some but not all of the lawyers and nonlawyers who helped edit the book have been through divorces themselves. None of the Wilsons on the board of editors are related to each other.

Marriage and Divorce Law in South Carolina

A Layperson's Guide

SUMMARY TABLE OF CONTENTS

Chapter One
Creating a Marriage

Chapter Two
Altering or Ending a Marriage

Chapter Three
How Cases Proceed Through the Family Court
(Actions for Separate Support and Maintenance, Annulments, and Divorces)

Chapter Four
Issues That Frequently Arise
When a Marriage Ends

Chapter Five
Issues That Sometimes Arise After Divorce

Chapter Six
Hiring and Working with a Lawyer

INTRODUCTION

This book provides some basic information about marriage and divorce law in South Carolina. It is intended to be a complement to legal advice and other professional services, not a substitute for them.

Divorce is a fact of life in America, and very few people go through life without being affected by divorce in some significant way. Fortunately, the laws that govern the dissolution of marriages have become increasingly clear and fair, and the systems for processing divorces are more efficient than ever. Room for improvement remains, of course, but there are fewer inequities and inefficiencies to resolve in the future than have been resolved in the past.

Marriages and divorces are very complex events, each having unique facts and circumstances. As counselors, lawyers help clients make decisions. The function of a lawyer is to examine the facts and circumstances of each case in light of the law, then to provide information, advice, or projections to the client.

When a client is facing a decision, a lawyer can help the client understand the nature of the legal issues, determine the client's priorities, identify alternative solutions, anticipate the possible consequences of each alternative, and make the best possible decision. Once a decision is made, a lawyer can help the client take appropriate actions consistent with that decision. This book cannot perform any of those functions of lawyers; it can only provide some information that might be relevant to decisions about marriage and divorce.

There are three primary sources of law: common law, statutory law, and case law. The common law of England established many principles of law that remain valid today. In South Carolina, the common law governs the decisions of courts unless it has been changed by legislative or judicial action. Statutory laws are enacted by state legislatures or the U.S. Congress. Most marriage and divorce statutes are enacted by state legislatures, although there is a growing amount of federal legislation related to certain aspects of marital law. The appellate courts of South Carolina (the Supreme Court and the Court of Appeals) interpret and explain the meaning of the common law and South Carolina statutes in the context of particular cases. A decision of an appellate court becomes case law when it is published. This establishes "legal precedent" which the trial courts are expected to follow when they are confronted with similar facts in future cases.

Statutes and case law reflect the public policies and judicial philosophies of the legislators and judges of each state. These policies and philosophies are shaped by wide spectrums of political, social, historical, and religious realities, therefore, the rules and regulations about marriage and divorce vary from state to state, often quite significantly. Any statement in this book about marriage and divorce law in South Carolina is not intended to be a correct statement of the law of any other state. Although the author strived to ensure the accuracy of the information contained in this book at the time of its publication, marriage and divorce laws change frequently. No one should make any significant decisions about marriage or divorce in South Carolina without first consulting a lawyer who is licensed to practice law in South Carolina.

CHAPTER ONE

Creating a Marriage

Introduction to Marriage

No one can create a valid marriage without meeting the legal requirements for marriage. The validity of a marriage is determined by the laws of the place where the attempt to become married occurs. If a marriage is valid in the state or country where it was contracted, South Carolina will also recognize the marriage as valid, unless something about the marriage violates public policy.

People have many reasons for deciding to get married. Love is the most often cited reason. Economic theorists offer a less emotional justification for marriage. They suggest that each person conducts a cost-benefit analysis before deciding to marry. If a person believes that the benefits of being married will exceed the benefits of remaining single, that person will want to get married. People often conclude that marriage will offer more benefits than bachelorhood because marriage provides an opportunity for two people to combine their resources and labor, thus enabling them to produce more commodities than either one could produce alone. "Commodities" encompasses anything of value, including children, companionship, and sexual satisfaction. Once married, a person will remain married so long as that person believes that the expected benefits from remaining married are better than the expected benefits from either being single or remarrying someone else. Whatever their reasons for deciding to get married, most people begin marriage believing that theirs will last forever. Unfortunately, a high percentage of marriages end in divorce.

Breach of Promise to Marry

South Carolina still recognizes a cause of action for breach of promise to marry. This means that if someone breaks a promise to marry, that person can be held responsible for any financial damage that the broken promise causes.

The plaintiff is entitled to compensatory damages such as would place her in as good a position as if the contract had been performed. These damages may include compensation for pain and suffering, mortification, humiliation suffered and injury to the health or psyche. The plaintiff may also recover for the loss of pecuniary and social advantages of the promised marriage.

The plaintiff may also recover expenditures made in preparation of the marriage. Additionally, if the plaintiff withdraws from employment in reliance on the marriage contract, the defendant is liable for wages lost as a direct consequence. Likewise, compensation for loss of reputation has been held recoverable in breach of promise actions.[1]

Engagement Rings

An engagement ring must be returned when an engagement is broken, regardless of who was at fault in ending the engagement. The rule is not the same in every state.

An engagement ring by its very nature is a symbol of the donor's continuing devotion to the donee. Once an engagement is cancelled, the ring no longer holds that significance. Thus, if a party presents evidence that a ring was given in contemplation of marriage, the ring is an engagement ring. As an engagement ring, the gift is

---

[1] Source: Suzanne E. Coe, *Breach of Promise to Marry*, 6 S.C. Jur. § 12 (2015).

impliedly conditioned upon the marriage taking place. Until the condition underlying the gift is fulfilled, the attempted gift is unenforceable and must be returned to the donor upon the donor's request.

Premarital Agreements

Premarital agreements (also called antenuptial or prenuptial agreements) are agreements between prospective spouses made in contemplation of marriage. They become effective only upon marriage.

The use of premarital agreements is growing in popularity as the divorce rate increases, especially among people entering second marriages. Premarital agreements are full of risks, however. When two people are contemplating marriage, they do not expect their marriage ever to fail, therefore, they do not believe that the terms of a premarital agreement will ever become important. The reality is that many marriages do fail, and it is impossible to anticipate going into a marriage what circumstances will exist when failure occurs. No one should sign a premarital agreement without consulting a lawyer. Premarital agreements are complex and dangerous contracts with potentially disastrous legal consequences for the unwary.

South Carolina law about premarital agreements is still somewhat undeveloped. A statute provides that premarital agreements can be used to designate that property belonging to one party before the marriage will continue to be that party's personal property after the marriage takes place. Until recently, it was less clear whether premarital agreements could be used to accomplish other objectives in South Carolina but a series of decisions by the appellate courts reflect a growing willingness to approve and enforce premarital agreements.

There are two types of issues that people may try to address in premarital contracts: the regulation of financial and other affairs between spouses during the marriage, or the resolution of matters in the event of separation or divorce. [Contracts dealing with personal matters between people who live together but do not marry are beyond the scope of this book. However, one should note that South Carolina law is unclear about the enforceability of such contracts. They may be deemed to violate public policy and be declared void.]

Premarital agreements that deal with the regulation of affairs between spouses during marriage will be upheld and enforced as a general rule, although agreements that affect the basic obligations of marriage may be deemed to be against public policy. The marriage contract is one in which the State of South Carolina takes a vital interest. Once entered into, the law imposes upon the parties certain mutual obligations and liabilities that have long been considered essential incidents to the marital relationship. These incidents to marriage are deemed vitally important to its preservation and stability. Thus, any agreement that has the effect of materially altering them as a condition of the relationship may be considered against public policy and, therefore, void. For example, it seemed well-established in South Carolina that an agreement between two spouses that they did not have an obligation to support each other during the marriage would be void, but the South Carolina Supreme Court created some uncertainty about this when it said in a 2003 case that "parties are free to contractually alter the obligations which would otherwise attach to marriage."

In the same case, the Supreme Court held that waivers of alimony in premarital agreements are not against public policy and will be enforced if the following conditions are met: (1) the agreement was not obtained through fraud, duress, or mistake, or through misrepresentation or nondisclosure of material facts; (2) the agreement is not unconscionable; and (3) the facts and circumstances have not changed since the agreement was executed, so as to make its enforcement unfair and unreasonable.

Statutory and Common Law Marriages Can be Created in South Carolina

A marriage can be created two ways in South Carolina. The first way is to obtain a license and participate in a wedding ceremony. The second way is to create a common law marriage. South Carolina is one of few states that still recognize common law marriages. The South Carolina legislature may abolish common law marriages at some point in the future. If it does, such action should not affect the validity of common law marriages that exist at that time.

Both forms of marriage (statutory and common law) are equally valid once they are created. Both involve the same rights and obligations, and both forms of marriage last until they are dissolved by death or court order. The only difference between common law and statutory marriages is the manner in which they are created. Statutory marriages require a marriage license and a marriage ceremony; common law marriages do not.

Creation of a common law marriage is simple. A valid common law marriage requires: (1) a mutually understood agreement of a man and woman to be married, (2) both having the capacity to marry, (3) accompanied or followed by cohabitation, and (4) the couple publicly representing themselves to be married. No fixed minimum time period of cohabitation is required to establish a common law marriage. The requirement that the parties must hold themselves out to the public as husband and wife has been satisfied by evidence such as the filing of joint tax returns, opening joint bank accounts with the husband's surname, and listing each other as husband and wife on children's birth certificates. Common law marriages do not require either a license or a ceremony.

South Carolina law requires any person who wants to contract matrimony within this state to first procure a license. However, South Carolina has a strong public policy in favor of marriage, therefore, even marriages that are contracted with an invalid license or without a license will be recognized as valid. This includes common law marriages.

South Carolina requires a twenty-four hour waiting period between the application for a license and its issuance. A probate judge or clerk of court will issue a marriage license upon the filing of the application, the lapse of twenty-four hours, the payment of a fee, and the filing of a sworn statement that the parties are legally entitled to marry (along with their full names, ages, and places of residence). South Carolina is one of few states that do not require a physical examination or blood test.

No marriage can be created unless both parties intend to be married. To create a valid statutory marriage, a man and a woman must make a formal declaration of their intent and willingness to be married in the presence of a person who is authorized to administer a marriage ceremony in South Carolina. Authorized persons include ministers of the Gospel, Jewish rabbis, and officers authorized to administer oaths (including notaries public). No ceremony or formal declaration of intent to be married is required to establish a valid common law marriage.

In light of the relative ease of creating a valid common law marriage, one could reasonably ask why anyone goes to the trouble to establish a statutory marriage. Part of the answer is tradition. Most people obtain a marriage license and go through a marriage ceremony. The ceremony presents an opportunity to celebrate the marriage with family and friends, and it marks a moment at which a man and a woman publically declare their mutual love and devotion. It serves as a punctuation mark, a clear statement that the parties intend to be husband and wife. Another reason for participating in a formal exchange of vows is that some religions require a ceremony before a marriage will be recognized by the church.

An important reason to create a statutory rather than a common law marriage is that a permanent record of the marriage is created when the marriage license is filed after the ceremony with the Bureau of Vital Statistics of the Department of Health and Environmental Control (DHEC). Vital statistics records can be used to prove the existence of a marriage and when it was created. This can be very important after someone dies, particularly if more than one person claims to be married to the deceased person and seeks to inherit a portion of the deceased person's estate. Proving the existence of a common law marriage or refuting another person's claim of common law marriage may be very difficult, especially since a key witness has died.

There is a way for people living in common law marriages to establish a record of the marriage. A state law allows an official record of a marriage to be established by filing an affidavit of two or more reputable persons who were informed of the marriage and have knowledge that the persons so claiming to be married have lived together as husband and wife. The affidavit is to be filed with the official whose duty it is to record marriages in the county in which the marriage was contracted. Not many people in common law marriages take advantage of this option, perhaps because those who are inclined to make a record of their marriage choose the marriage license and formal declaration route.

A marriage contract in South Carolina (statutory or common law) is not final until it is consummated by cohabitation. Cohabitation is considered to be evidence of the mutual consent required to create any valid contract. If the parties have not cohabited, the lack of consent of either party will be inferred and the marriage is voidable, that is, either party could seek to annul the marriage during their lifetimes.

The precise meaning of "cohabitation" is not defined in either statutory or case law. Clearly, a vital element of cohabitation is residing together in the same home, at least for a short period of time. Less clear is whether or not any sexual activity is required before the parties will be deemed to have cohabited. Even if the parties have not engaged in sexual intercourse (coition), some degree of sexual intimacy short of intercourse may be required to consummate the marriage. Simply living in the same house may not be enough, but this is an unresolved issue of law in South Carolina.

Cohabitation alone does not create a common law marriage. The difference between marriage and concubinage rests in the intent of the cohabiting parties. The intent in marriage consists of living together by agreement of a man and woman as husband and wife. The intent in concubinage consists of a man and woman living together in the contrary fashion. However, the existence of a common law marriage may be inferred from evidence of well-established and long-continued cohabitation, even in the face of testimony that no express agreement to be married was ever made. There is a strong presumption in favor of marriage by cohabitation, apparently matrimonial, coupled with social acceptance over a long period of time. A man and woman living together as husband and wife are generally presumed under the law to be married, if they have acquired a reputation as a married couple. While the presumption of marriage from cohabitation and reputation is ordinarily a rebuttable presumption, the degree of proof to overcome it is generally very high, especially where the parties have cohabited as husband and wife for a long time. Thus, the necessary agreement may be inferred under some circumstances from the nature and duration of open cohabitation. On the other hand, living together for a short duration of time is not likely to create a common law marriage, absent clear evidence of the parties' intention to be married and some representation to the public that two people intend to be married.

Who Does Not Have the Capacity to Get Married in South Carolina

All persons may lawfully contract matrimony, except mentally incompetent persons and any persons who are prohibited from marriage, who include people who are too closely related by blood or marriage, anyone who is already married, and females and males younger than 16.

Mentally Incompetent People

Mentally incompetent persons may not lawfully contract marriage. A South Carolina statute provides, however, that a mental patient who has not been adjudicated to be an incompetent person cannot be denied the right to marry. This right to marry would logically extend to people who are not mental patients. The key question is whether the person understood the nature of his or her actions when the marriage vows were made. One case in South Carolina describes the standard as follows: "Mere weakness or imbecility of mind is not sufficient, nor eccentricity or partial dementia, but it must be such a derangement as prevents the party from comprehending the nature of the contract and from giving to it his free and intelligent consent in order to warrant a decree nullifying the purported marriage."

The mental incompetency must exist at the time of marriage to invalidate the marriage. Marriages by mentally incompetent people in South Carolina are voidable rather than void. Persons who suffer from lunacy at the time of marriage may consummate - or validate - their marriages during a lucid period.

People Who Are Too Closely Related

People who are closely related by blood (consanguinity) or marriage (affinity) are prohibited from marrying. First cousins may marry each other in South Carolina, but a man cannot marry the following people to whom he is too closely related by blood: his mother, grandmother, daughter, granddaughter, sister, niece, or aunt. Nor can he marry the following people to whom he is related by marriage, even after his marriage and theirs have ended: his stepmother, grandfather's wife, son's wife, grandson's wife, wife's mother, wife's grandmother, wife's daughter, or wife's granddaughter. The same prohibitions apply to women. Case law extends these restrictions to relations of the half blood, such as half sisters.

A marriage to someone within the prohibited degrees of relationship is voidable, not void. A voidable marriage can only be attacked by the parties to the marriage and only during their lifetimes. If the marriage is not voided during the lives of the spouses, it is considered valid in all respects for civil purposes.

Anyone who is considering a marriage to someone within the degrees of relationship prohibited by law should seek legal advice regarding potential criminal issues. South Carolina law makes it a crime to engage in sexual intercourse with someone within the prohibited degrees of affinity and consanguinity. The penalty for violation of the incest law is not less than a $500 fine or one year in jail or both. It is not clear if the criminal statute would apply where the parties are married, or whether local prosecutors would use the statute against married persons. However, legal advice should be obtained before entering marriage with someone within the scope of the affinity and consanguinity laws.

Anyone Who Is Already Married

South Carolinians can only have one spouse at a time. All marriages contracted while either of the parties has a living wife or husband are void. A void marriage cannot be ratified or confirmed and thereby made valid. However, in keeping with the state's policy to promote and maintain the institution of marriage, South Carolina courts will assume a second marriage is valid until the existence of a preceding spouse is proved.

A South Carolina statute provides some protection to people who remarry more than five years after a husband or wife is absent. The statute creates a presumption of death of the first spouse that will prevail over any presumption of continuance of life, in the absence of evidence to rebut the presumption. A spouse wishing to rely on this statute must meet two requirements. First, he or she cannot abandon a spouse, leave the jurisdiction, remarry, and then use the section as a shield to protect the second marriage. A continuous unexplained five-year absence creates a presumption of death, but such a presumption "will not be indulged for the benefit of one who deserts his former spouse." Second, the abandoned or deserted spouse must also make a good faith effort to ascertain the whereabouts of the abandoning or deserting spouse.

The risk of having a missing spouse return and disrupt the second marriage can be avoided by obtaining a judicial declaration of presumed death by establishing that an absent spouse has not been heard from for seven years.[2] If a declaration of presumed death is

---

[2] Yes, there is a discrepancy that has no apparent rational basis. The presumption of death arises after five years, but one must wait seven years to obtain a judicial declaration of presumed death.

obtained, the reappearance or return of the absent spouse shall not alter such adjudication or invalidate or upset any subsequent marriage entered into by the abandoned spouse.

Another pitfall of the bigamous marriage is the criminal sanction against it. Conviction of bigamy could result in a penalty of from six months to five years in the penitentiary or six months in jail and a fine of not less than $500.

People Who Are Too Young to Marry

A marriage contracted by a male or female younger than 16 is void *ab initio*. That is, it cannot exist.

A marriage license cannot be issued to a person under the age of 16. Furthermore, the consent of an adult is required before a marriage license can be issued to a person younger than 18. If an applicant is younger than 18 and resides with father, mother, or other relative or guardian, a license will not be issued until the person from whom the license is requested is furnished with a sworn affidavit by such father, mother, or other relative or guardian giving his or her consent to the marriage.

Parental consent is not required to obtain a marriage license before reaching 18 if a female applicant is pregnant or has given birth to a child (and this fact is documented by a physician), if the proposed marriage is to the presumed father of the child. A variety of other people are authorized by statute to consent to the female's marriage (including the superintendent of the county department of social services). No consent to the marriage of the presumed father is required.

Statutory requirements for consent to obtain a marriage license before the age of 18 are completely defeated by the fact that marriage licenses are not required to create common law marriages, which can be created at the age of 16 without anyone's consent other than the parties to the marriage. (Before August 17, 2000, valid common law marriages could be contracted when females were 14 and males were 16. Before June 11, 1997, valid common law marriages could be contracted when females were 12 and males were 14, and voidable common law marriages could be contracted as young as seven years old.)

The Legal Significance of Being Married

Marriage is both a status and a contract. It resembles a contract because a marriage cannot exist unless two people agree to be married. It is unlike most contracts because many of the most important rights and obligations of the relationship are imposed by law, not by agreement, and the marriage cannot be ended without a court order. Married people who have the status of "being married" are treated differently by the law in many ways from those who are not married.

Cohabitation

One South Carolina judge described the rights and duties of marriage to include "consortium, i.e., the conjugal society, comfort, companionship, and affection of each other." Marriage creates a right and a duty for two people to live together, absent a mutual agreement to live apart or sufficient justification for one party to refuse to live with the other. You cannot physically force a spouse to continue living with you, but an unjustified refusal to live with one's spouse may constitute desertion, a ground for divorce.

Sexual Intercourse

Married people have the right to engage in sexual intercourse with each other, but not with anyone else. It is a crime in South Carolina for people who are not married to cohabit or engage in intercourse on a regular basis. A statute enacted about 100 years ago makes fornication a crime punishable by a fine of from $100 to $500, or imprisonment for from six months to one year, or both.

The crime of fornication is defined as "the living together and carnal intercourse with each other or habitual carnal intercourse with each other without living together of a man and a woman, both being unmarried." Thus, regular or habitual fornication is the key for the criminal offense. How much repetition is required? The last case to consider this was in 1889, in which the Supreme Court of South Carolina approved a jury charge that basically held that the acts of intercourse involved must be "frequent, not occasional," and otherwise left things up to the jury. Prosecutions for the crime of fornication are not frequently undertaken, but they have occurred. Prosecution is left to the discretion of the Solicitor for each judicial circuit.

The law does not impose an obligation on either spouse to engage in sexual intercourse, although marriage creates a legal right and a social expectation that couples will do so. Even under the common law, there was a duty to refrain from intercourse if the other spouse reasonably requested forbearance. Today, a spouse who physically forces the other spouse to engage in sexual intercourse would be guilty of the crime of spousal sexual battery and perhaps other crimes. The offending spouse's conduct must be reported to appropriate law enforcement authorities within 30 days in order for a spouse to be prosecuted for this offense.

Mutual Support

Husbands and wives have a duty to support each other financially. Any able-bodied person capable of earning a livelihood is, regardless of gender, responsible for the "reasonable support" of his or her spouse and minor children. Failure to provide such support is a criminal misdemeanor punishable by fine, imprisonment, or both.

Prosecutions under this law are rare, however. It is more common for spousal and child support to be pursued through the Family Court during divorce or separate support and maintenance actions or as separate child support actions.

Confidentiality

Communications between spouses are confidential. No husband or wife may be required to disclose any confidential or, in a criminal proceeding, any communication made by one to the other during their marriage, except in cases involving child abuse. South Carolina law is a bit unusual, however, because the testifying spouse holds the privilege, not the spouse who made the communication. Thus, if one spouse chooses to testify against his or her spouse, the other spouse may not be able to prevent it.

Common Last Name

There is no requirement in South Carolina that married people have the same surname, although they may if they wish. The law seems to allow any two people to choose to have a common last name irrespective of whether or not they are married. If people choose to share a surname, it does not have to be either of their previous surnames. They can pick any name they desire, and they can change it whenever they want. This freedom does not appear to be available to minors, except those who get married before they are 18.

Although the law does not require judicial approval or any other documentation of name changes, most people prefer to have legal proof that their names have changed. Several types of legal proof include a marriage license, a divorce decree, or an independent order of the Family Court granting a petition for a name change.

Assets and Debts

The law considers marriage to be an economic partnership. Thus, assets acquired during the marriage usually belong to both spouses, irrespective of which spouse acquired them or whose name is on the title to the property. (See the chapter on property for more information about the division of marital property.)

Generally, assets and debts acquired prior to marriage remain the separate responsibility of the spouse who acquired them unless some conduct or expression of intent by the parties creates a joint interest. Although the Family Court has the authority to apportion debts between the parties to a divorce action, debts acquired by one spouse during the marriage are not the responsibility of the other spouse, unless the debt is for a product or a service that is considered "necessary." The Doctrine of Necessaries is an important concept in South Carolina. The Doctrine provides that one spouse may be liable for the other spouse's debts that were contracted prior to or during the marriage, if the goods or services provided to the spouse were "necessary" for the support of the spouse or their minor children residing with them. A third party who provides necessary goods or services to either spouse may bring an action for recovery against both spouses. Necessary services may include, for example, the costs of medical care.

Inheritance Rights

The surviving spouse of a person who dies intestate (without a will) is entitled to a share of the decedent's estate. If there is no surviving child of the decedent, the spouse is entitled to the entire intestate estate. If there are one or more surviving children, the spouse receives one-half of the intestate estate.

One spouse cannot prevent the other spouse from inheriting part of the estate by excluding the other spouse from the will.

Surviving spouses of decedents who are domiciled at the time of death in South Carolina may claim an "elective share" of the decedent's estate even if the will excludes them. An "elective share" means the surviving spouse can accept what the deceased spouse left in the will, if anything, or can elect to take one-third of the value of the estate, but not both. The election must occur within eight months after the decedent's death or six months after the probate of the decedent's will.

If a person fails to provide in a will for a spouse married after the execution of the will, the omitted spouse shall receive the same share that he or she would have received if the decedent had died intestate, unless the will shows the omission to be intentional, or unless the testator provided for the spouse outside the will with the intention that the nontestamentary provisions be instead of any gifts under the will.

Children

> ## Legitimacy

Children are deemed to be legitimate or illegitimate on the basis of whether their parents were married at the time they were conceived or born. The legal consequences of being born out of wedlock are virtually nonexistent, although they were once quite severe.

Parents of illegitimate children are required to support them the same as children born during wedlock.

A child born out of wedlock becomes just as "legitimate" as if the child was born in lawful wedlock if the child's parents marry at any time, even after the child is born. An illegitimate child will not, however, be legitimized merely because the child's natural mother marries someone. It must be the child's biological father. The child becomes eligible to inherit from both parents once the parents marry.

Illegitimate children are also allowed to claim a share of their fathers' estates if paternity is established by a court of law. However, the court action to establish paternity must be commenced before the death of the father or within the later of eight months after the death of the father or six months after the probate of his estate. Paternity established by adjudication does not qualify the father or his kindred to inherit from or through the child unless the father has openly treated the child as his and has not refused to support the child.

➢ Care, Education, and Welfare

The respective rights of parents regarding the care, education, and control of children involve very complex issues of law, irrespective of whether the parents are married. (For additional information see the sections on child custody and support in Chapter Four.)

Married and unmarried parents are equally charged with the welfare and education of their minor children, along with the care and management of the children's estates.

➢ Children's Names

Parents have a right to give their children any surnames (last names) they wish to give, just as they determine their children's given names. However, one parent cannot unilaterally change a child's last name after a divorce, unless a Family Court judge determines that the change would be in the child's best interests.

When the parents of a child are not married, both parents have an equal interest in their children bearing their respective surnames. If the parents cannot agree on which surname to give their children, a Family Court judge can resolve their dispute by examining a range of factors to determine what would be in the children's best interest.

CHAPTER TWO

Altering or Ending a Marriage

The Psychological Stages of Divorce

Our society makes marriage easy to get into but difficult to get out of. Getting married is almost always one of the happiest, most enjoyable events in life. Ending a marriage is frequently the opposite. Divorces are tragic events that produce strong emotions and create very difficult personal and societal problems. No one ever really wins in a divorce, not even the lawyers.

The psychodynamics of divorce are very complex. Divorce is an emotional experience that can have significant psychological consequences.

Why do people get divorced? Long-term marriages depend in large part on three factors: willingness on the part of both spouses to change in response to each other, willingness to tolerate each other's imperfections, and sharing the same values (including religious values).

Each marriage is different, and when a marriage fails it is never for any single reason. Some psychologists believe that the best general explanation is that people get divorced because they no longer meet each other's needs. People enter marriage with certain expectations. Sometimes these expectations are unrealistic. Sometimes the expectations change or the willingness of the marital partner to help meet those expectations changes. Sometimes one spouse meets another person who seems to be a potentially better partner in marriage. In any event, marital relationships tend to go bad when there is a mismatch between what one spouse wants from the marriage and what that spouse thinks he or she is actually getting out of the marriage. Economic theorists would say that divorce occurs when a married person concludes that the expected benefits from remaining married are not as good as the expected benefits from either being single or marrying someone else.

There are identifiable emotional phases that people typically encounter during the divorce process.[3] Psychologists disagree among themselves about the exact number of phases a person experiences during a divorce or what label to put on each phase, but they essentially agree about the basic emotional realities of divorce. The following discussion of psychological stages assumes there is a clearly identifiable "initiator" of the divorce and that the other spouse does not expect or want a divorce, at least at the outset. This is the situation in 85% of divorces, whereas 15% arise from a mutual desire to end the marriage.

It should be noted that the emotional phases of divorce do not occur in an orderly manner. They can overlap and they can occur simultaneously. Regression is possible. Additional complexities are created by the fact that both spouses are frequently not in the same stage at the same time.

The first phase begins when one spouse begins thinking about the possibility of a divorce and ultimately raises the idea. This is the deliberation phase. People in this phase do not usually understand what is happening. Communication becomes less open and, typically, the fact that the marriage is in trouble is not verbalized directly. The spouse who is not the initiator denies there are serious problems with

---

[3] This section is adapted from Geoffrey Hamilton, Esq., and Thomas Merrill, Ph.D., *Why is My Client Nuts? . . . An Inquiry into the Psychodynamics of Divorce*, ABA SECTION OF FAMILY LAW 1989 ANNUAL MEETING COMPENDIUM 4 (1989).

the marriage and often blames existing problems on the other spouse. Some try to ignore it and do nothing, hoping the issue will simply go away. (Once the divorce is over, on the other hand, a substantial majority of divorced people feel that getting divorced was the right thing to do.)

Although the parties commonly do not discuss their feelings with each other, especially at the beginning of the deliberation phase, there are obvious changes in their relationship. One or both spouses frequently engage in indirect, covert, destructive behavior. Their sexual relationship breaks down, and they may begin sleeping in different bedrooms. The initiator may have an affair. The initiator "rewrites" the history of the marriage, primarily to justify the decision to break up.

The deliberation phase can go on for one or two years. Many people, of course, eventually decide not to seek a divorce. They weigh the pros and cons of marriage versus divorce, and sometimes renegotiate their relationship and reconcile their problems. Marriage counseling sometimes helps save marriages during the deliberation phase. In other cases, however, the initiator or both spouses reach a point of "no return," and the relationship moves toward the inevitable point of separation and divorce.

The deliberation phase ends when one spouse tells the other spouse that he or she wants a divorce. This frequently produces a relatively short, but intense decision-making phase. Although the intent to get a divorce has been seriously communicated, the outcome remains in doubt. Family, friends, and others get involved with advice and opinions about what should have been done and what should be done now. The spouse who did not initiate the divorce frequently retaliates in some fashion, trying to deflect the pain of rejection, punish the initiator, derail the decision to divorce, or all three. Often, the initiator, stung by guilt or outcry from family or friends, loses motivation, reconsiders, and decides to remain married. If not, the parties move to the next phase.

The next phase is the transition phase. The parties physically separate at the end of the deliberation phase, but find it difficult to come to grips with the reality that the marriage is really ending and they are becoming emotionally and psychologically separated. This is especially difficult for people who have been married for a long time or have children. Some see half of themselves and their lives ending, an experience from which many never recover. This phase is when one or both spouses may engage in a wide range of "crazy" behavior. Sexual "acting out" is not uncommon for men and women. The transition phase typically lasts for six months or so. Unfortunately, this "crazy time" phase is also when most divorcing people are having to make important decisions with long-term implications for the quality of their lives, including their positions about child custody and property division.

The next phase generally corresponds to the actual processing of the divorce through the court system. It typically lasts a year but can last substantially longer. This is when divorcing partners begin to redefine their roles in life. It can be a time of positive personal growth or one of stagnation and despair, or both.

After the divorce is final, the parties can begin the healing phase of the divorce process. This is when emotional balance should return to normal. Heathy people put the divorce behind them and move on with their lives. This phase can take two or more years. Once a new level of stability is achieved, it often continues indefinitely. Unfortunately, some people never readjust to life outside of marriage and continue to have adjustment problems indefinitely.

Divorce is easier on the person who initiates it, on men, in short marriages, and when there are no children. People also cope better with divorce if they are able to provide sufficient support for themselves, and if they have family, friends, church, or others who can provide emotional support. There are divorce support groups in every community.

Happy people with high self-esteem are better able to survive the emotional impact of divorce. Self-esteem is related directly to how satisfied people are with three areas of their lives: work, play, and primary personal relationships. At least one spouse's self-esteem is put at risk in most divorces (usually both spouses'), and if a person whose marriage is breaking down is also having problems with the work or play aspect of life, that person may be at risk of not being able to function adequately.

Divorce is seldom easy on anyone. One study found that even after ten years one-half of divorced women and one-third of divorced men remain as intensely angry at their former spouses as they were at the commencement of divorce proceedings. The apparent key to happiness after ten years is having a successful second marriage.

Children have it the worst of all. Children frequently blame themselves for their parents' divorces. Some will try to take on inappropriate roles including advising or nurturing one or both parents. The long-term impact seems to be a reluctance to allow themselves as adults to end up like their parents. They often carry the baggage of their parents' divorces into their own courtships and marriages. They view relationships as impermanent, unstable, and threatening, and they consequently have trouble maintaining committed relationships. A 1997 study found that it is usually better for children for their parents to stay in a bad marriage than to divorce. It seems that two parents, even if unhappy, are better than one when it comes to the emotional health of children. The exception to this is when marriages involve a high degree of conflict between the parents, but only about 30% of marriages that go sour involve high conflict situations that will harm children more than divorce.

One effort to reduce the impact of divorce on children is the development of programs that try to educate parents about the effects of divorce on children and how they can minimize the damage. In South Carolina, some counties are experimenting with pilot programs. There are some variations among the programs, but the general idea is the same: parents who are separated or divorced are encouraged to attend weekly educational, supportive classes that teach them about the divorce transition's effects on the entire family system. The programs also teach the special parenting skills needed by parents to help their children adjust to divorce.

Initial Things to Consider Upon Deciding to End a Marriage

Introduction

A decision to end a marriage will eventually lead to the Family Court because the <u>only</u> way to end a marriage in South Carolina is to obtain an order from the Family Court that grants a request to be divorced. Before that stage of the process is reached, however, people who have decided to separate or divorce must make many decisions. There is no such thing as a simple divorce. The undoing of every marriage involves making important, and frequently difficult, decisions about interpersonal relationships and economic entanglements.

One decision is whether to hire a lawyer and when. This topic is dealt with in some detail in Chapter Six. For most people, it would be a good idea to seek information from a lawyer as early in the process as possible, even before making a decision to separate or to seek a divorce.

Separating

Separation typically occurs shortly after one spouse expresses a desire to end the marriage. Physical separation often happens quickly, without the involvement of any lawyers or judges. However, a decision to move out of the marital home can have significant legal consequences. If either spouse moves out of the marital home against the wishes of the other and without adequate justification, there is a risk that he or she will be considered a deserter and, perhaps, jeopardize his or her legal rights, including the possibility of receiving spousal support. Similarly, a spouse who forcefully evicts the other spouse without reasonable cause, by changing the locks to the house or otherwise, would very likely be deemed to be the deserting spouse or, at least, be seen as coming to the Court with "unclean hands."

Even if one spouse has good reasons for moving out of the marital home, there is a risk that a Family Court judge will adopt the *status quo* at a temporary hearing and decide to let the other spouse continue living in the marital home until the final divorce hearing, which might not take place for more than a year. A divorcing parent who intends to seek custody of the children may face these choices: either vacate the home, taking the children and thereby cause additional disruption in the children's lives; vacate the home and abandon the children to the other spouse, at least temporarily; or continue in the marriage. None of these may be acceptable or viable options.

Sometimes, neither party is willing to move out of the marital home. This may happen because neither person has anywhere else to live, both are being obstinate, or they are afraid that moving out will disadvantage them in the divorce proceeding, especially if child custody is contested. The fear of being disadvantaged is not unfounded. If one parent moves out of the marital home, leaving the children and the other spouse behind, a Family Court judge may view this as a lack of commitment to the children and a sign that the parent who moves out believes that the other parent is capable of taking care of the children. In close cases, this could make a difference.

Whatever the reason why one spouse wants a divorce, a decision to continue living together after at least one spouse has decided to end the marriage is not a good thing. The dissolution of a marriage is a very stressful event in its initial stages even when people are able to physically separate. A decision to continue living in the same home will add more stress and increase the risk that conflicts and hostility will escalate and lead to emotional, if not physical, harm.

A refusal of both spouses to move out of the marital home creates a legal dilemma because both parties to a marriage generally have an equal right to live in the marital home regardless of whose name is on the lease or title. If one spouse is abusing the other spouse, the Protection From Domestic Abuse statute provides a quick way to get the abusive spouse out of the home (see Chapter Four). Otherwise, there is no fast way to force one party to move out.

The Family Court may hear divorce cases that are based on adultery, habitual drunkenness, or physical cruelty even if the parties are still living in the same house at the time the action is commenced. Otherwise, if courts were to require physical separation of the parties in order to bring a divorce action, divorcing parents who seek custody of their children would have these choices: either vacate the home, taking the children with them and thereby cause additional disruption in the children's lives; vacate the home and abandon the children to their spouse; or stay in the home and suffer the consequences. The Supreme Court of South Carolina has held that public policy permits a spouse to remain in the home and begin divorce litigation premised on fault grounds other than desertion. In such cases, the living arrangements of the parties and the children during the pendency of the litigation should be decided at the temporary hearing.

If none of the fault grounds for divorce exists, the parties must be living in separate residences before either of them can file an action for separate support and maintenance or divorce.

When neither spouse is willing to move out of the marital home, the best solution is for both spouses to hire lawyers who can help them reach an agreement as fast as possible about any issues that are in dispute between them, including who will live in the marital home while the divorce is going forward. Absent a fast agreement, the lawyers can at least initiate court proceedings that may or may not produce a court order about the use of the marital home in a few weeks or months.

Reducing Harm to Children

Divorces harm children, no matter their ages – even adult children. Children usually do not understand why parents cannot continue living together, and they sometimes blame themselves for causing the divorce. Too often, divorcing couples get so caught up in the turmoil of divorce that they forget about the importance of protecting their children until it is too late. If you have children and you are going through a divorce or contemplating one, you should see a professional marriage counselor or psychologist for advice about how to minimize the harm that the divorce will cause your children and to determine whether your children may need professional counseling.

There are some basic do's and don't's:

- ▸ do tell your children that they are not the cause of the divorce (don't assume they know).

- ▸ do reassure them that both parents still love them and that they will still have both parents after the divorce.

- do give the children your full attention, as difficult as that is under the circumstances.

- do everything possible to be friendly, collaborative, and accommodating toward your spouse when it involves the children.

- do not say bad things about your spouse.

- do not have arguments in front of the children.

- do not use the children as messengers between you and your spouse about anything to do with the divorce.

- do not use the children as spies to find out what your spouse is doing, thinking, saying, or spending.

- do not ask the children to take sides on any issue.

- do not use the children as counselors or otherwise confide in them about your problems.

- do not use the children as weapons for getting revenge on your spouse.

- do not use the children as leverage or "bargaining chips" in divorce settlement negotiations.

If there is a risk of physical violence to you or the children, refer to the section on violence in Chapter Four.

Dating and Socializing

You remain married until a Family Court judge signs a divorce decree and files it with the Clerk of the Family Court. If you date after separating, your spouse may try to use it against you. If you are thinking about asking for alimony, being sexually intimate with someone other than your spouse during the separation may bar you from getting any (see the section in this chapter on adultery).

If you receive an award of temporary alimony, and it is later proven that you committed adultery before or after the separation from your spouse, you may be required to repay all of the temporary alimony that you received after committing adultery.

A written agreement that "neither party will use adultery as a bar to alimony" may be upheld as a valid waiver of a right and used to prevent either party from claiming that adultery should prevent an award of alimony.

If you want custody of your children, be aware that who you date, how often you date or otherwise socialize, and what you do on these occasions could have an impact on a judge's opinion of which parent is best suited to have custody (see the section in this chapter on child custody). If you date while your divorce action is pending, you also risk angering your spouse, thereby jeopardizing your spouse's willingness to be reasonable in settlement negotiations. You should not introduce your children to a new romantic interest in your life during the divorce process. You should seek advice of a lawyer about how dating and socializing might affect your divorce.

Making Agreements

You should talk to a lawyer before making any agreements with your spouse. You don't have to hire the lawyer to represent you through the entire process, but you need to understand your legal rights before you make any agreements. Whatever you do, you should seek a lawyer's advice before signing anything.

Spending some money up front on a lawyer will likely save you more money in the long run. A lawyer can advise you about your rights and options with respect to your immediate problems, and a lawyer can help you anticipate and deal with issues that might arise much later. A thoughtfully prepared separation agreement will reduce the likelihood of having to engage in expensive contested litigation now or in the future.

Very few issues in divorces are decided by a Family Court judge. In the great majority of divorce cases, the Family Court judge does nothing more than approve the agreements of parties in a divorce action and review the sufficiency of evidence establishing that the parties have lived separate and apart without cohabitation for more than a year. Most divorce hearings take fifteen minutes or less. This is because the parties themselves have worked out the details of their divorce, usually with the assistance of their lawyers. Even when a Family Court judge is required to resolve a dispute, it usually involves only a few issues that the parties have not been able to decide themselves.

Many people work out the details of their divorces quickly and without much conflict. Some, unfortunately, find it impossible to work things out at all. The worst conflicts occur when people cannot agree on child custody, and people with substantial assets will sometimes fight for years over how to divide their money and property.

If people can agree, there is no legal requirement that the agreement take any particular form. If they wish, people who want to end their marriages can simply decide what they want to do, then do it. They can even decide who will have custody of the children and how much child support will be paid. There is no law that requires them to have lawyers or to seek court approval of their agreements. The Family Court will only get involved if one or both of the parties asks it to help resolve a dispute or to approve an agreement. The only thing that cannot be accomplished by agreement of the parties is to get divorced. Only a Family Court order can accomplish that.

Although the law does not require people to formalize the agreements they make during the divorce process, it may be a good idea to do so. This is particularly true regarding agreements about child custody and support. Court approval of child custody agreements creates legal rights for the custodial and noncustodial parents, and it reduces the possibility of future litigation. If parents reach an agreement about child support that requires the noncustodial parent to pay an amount that is less than the South Carolina Child Support Guidelines would require, the child could come back years later and try to recover retroactive child support from the noncustodial parent, unless the Family Court has approved the child support arrangement.

The Family Court is required to consider the overall fairness of any agreements that are submitted for its approval. This is to protect against the possibility that one spouse will convince the other to agree to terms that are clearly unfair.

Another reason to formalize agreements during the divorce process is to ensure the probability that they will be enforceable if either party decides not to comply with the agreement. As a general proposition, Family Courts are less inclined to uphold agreements made between a divorcing husband and wife if either of them entered into the agreement without first obtaining advice from a lawyer.

Similarly, Family Courts are more inclined to approve and enforce agreements about property division and other financial matters if both parties make fair disclosure to each other about their assets and liabilities.

If an agreement is signed that is not submitted to the Family Court for approval during the divorce process, it may still be an enforceable contract. If a problem arises in the future, however, disputes about the contract may have to be litigated in the Circuit Court of Common Pleas, not the Family Court, depending on the language in the agreement. The exception to this is that the Family Court has exclusive jurisdiction over matters involving minor children that cannot be affected by an agreement between their parents.

Maintaining Reasonable Access to Joint Assets

It is difficult to predict exactly how a spouse will react once he or she makes a decision to end the marriage or learns that the other spouse wants to end the marriage. Some people going through a divorce are surprised to learn that their spouses will no longer help make payments on the mortgage or pay for other living expenses. Others discover that their spouses have cleaned out safe deposit boxes and joint bank accounts, packed up the best furniture and moved it out of the marital home, and taken one car and sold the other.

It is clear that when one spouse seizes or disposes of joint assets for the purpose of depriving the other spouse of reasonable access to those assets, the Family Court will deal harshly with that person once the case gets to court. While waiting for this to happen, however, life can be very hard for a spouse who is left without support, assets, useful furnishings, or transportation.

Both spouses should work together to ensure that they will both have reasonable access to jointly owned assets until their property is divided by agreement or by the Family Court. If one spouse suspects that the other might try to seize control of the assets and deny fair access to them, however, it may be appropriate to consider seizing control of the assets first, but only for the purpose of ensuring reasonable access to them by both spouses. For example, it might be appropriate to close a joint banking account and either give half of it to the other spouse or provide the other spouse with access to the funds in some other way. If one spouse remains in the marital home, it might make sense to change the door locks to control access by the other spouse. Prompt notice to the other spouse of what has happened and why is not only the right thing to do, but it will also reduce the risk of escalating hostilities or angering a Family Court judge. It would be prudent to obtain the advice of a lawyer before taking control of jointly owned assets, if time permits.

One of the first things that should be done after making a decision to end the marriage (or learning that your spouse wants a divorce) is to cancel any joint credit cards and joint charge accounts, or at least lower the credit limit to within $100 of the current balances. There is seldom a good reason to take a risk that the other spouse will run up charges on joint accounts for which you might be held responsible. If asked to do it, the Family Court will allocate the responsibility for credit card and other debts between divorcing spouses. However, even if the Family Court's allocation of responsibility for debts makes one spouse responsible for paying off a credit card debt, the Court's order does not affect the credit card company's right to pursue anyone who co-signed the credit card application and agreed to be responsible for the bill. If the person who was ordered by the Family Court to make the payments does not do so, he or she may be held in contempt of court (unless, perhaps, that spouse files for bankruptcy), but the credit card company can still legally pursue collection from the other co-signer.

If you are solely responsible for a credit card account, but your spouse has a card that is charged to the account, ask for the card. If your spouse refuses to give it to you, ask the credit card company to cancel the card and send you a new card with a different account number.

Gathering Evidence

If you think there might be any disputed issues during the divorce proceedings, you will need evidence to present to the Family Court. Evidence can be the testimony of the parties or other people who have something relevant to say, and it can be documents that have something to do with the matters before the Court. Any person who is considering divorce should think about collecting evidence as soon as possible.

To reduce the risk of wasting time and money in the pursuit of evidence, it would be wise to seek legal advice about what evidence will be most relevant to the issues in your divorce and about the most efficient ways to gather it. The following suggestions are provided for people who are not able to seek legal advice. The kinds of evidence you will need depend on the issues that might be in dispute, but you can expect the following to be helpful in most cases:

- ▸ paycheck stubs.

- ▸ copies of recent income tax returns.

- ▸ financial statements, e.g., from banks and investment firms.

- ▸ completed loan applications.

- ▸ canceled checks and check registers.

- ▸ monthly bills and credit card statements.

- ▸ information about retirement plans and IRA's.

- ▸ deeds.

- ▸ property tax receipts and appraisals.

- ▸ insurance policies.

- ▸ any written agreements or notes between you and your spouse.

If you intend to convince a Family Court judge that your spouse committed adultery, you will need more than your suspicions, and perhaps even more than your spouse's confession. If all you have are suspicions, a starting point is to write down all of the things that caused you to suspect your spouse of adultery. If you have letters or other written notes between your spouse and the suspected paramour, these might be evidence that the Family Court will accept.

One thing that you should not do is to tape record telephone conversations between your spouse and a suspected paramour. This is called "wiretapping" which is not only a federal criminal offense, but it is also a violation of your spouse's and the paramour's right to privacy which would give them a basis for suing you for damages in Federal Court. Worst of all, the tape would probably not even be admissible as evidence in the Family Court, nor would any evidence that it led to. You can tape your own conversations with other people, but no one can tape conversations between other people unless one of them has given prior consent. A custodial parent can record a minor child's conversations with other people, including the noncustodial parent, but the parent must have a good faith, objectively reasonable basis for believing that it is necessary and in the best interests of the child.

Federal and state laws are rapidly evolving regarding what one can and cannot do with another person's email, social media, and computers or other electronic devices. It is against the law to open another person's mail or to access incoming e-mail messages that are not addressed to you. It is a violation of law to access someone's stored emails that are in electronic storage, e.g., in a Yahoo account, without authorization. Federal and state criminal and civil penalties can be imposed. You should consult with a lawyer before accessing any equipment or accounts belonging to another person. You should also consult with a lawyer before installing any spyware on a family computer or someone else's personal computer.

If you have friends who saw suspicious conduct between your spouse and a paramour or to whom your spouse or the paramour admitted committing adultery, their testimony about what they saw and what was said could be used as evidence in the Family Court.

A traditional way to obtain evidence of adultery is to hire a professional investigator who is not a relative or a personal friend of yours to follow your spouse. If this person observes conduct from which a Family Court judge would conclude that your spouse committed adultery, the investigator's testimony may be all that is needed to prove adultery. Private investigators are required to have detailed, signed, SLED-approved contracts with their clients. One source for finding private investigators is the South Carolina Association of Legal Investigators (SCALI). Its website is located at www.scalinv.com.

If you expect there will be disagreements about property division, you should find and secure any titles to the property. You should also secure any other documents that show what the property is worth as well as who paid for the property, made improvements to it, or otherwise contributed to its current value.

If child custody might be an issue, you should try to find witnesses or to collect or create documents that will help the Family Court determine which parent was the primary caretaker, especially if both parents worked during the marriage. This might include evidence showing who participated in school and other activities of the children and who took them to medical and other appointments. It will also be relevant to a custody decision if you have witnesses or documents that reflect badly on the moral character of your spouse or otherwise raise questions about your spouse's fitness to have custody.

When spousal support or child support is an issue in divorce proceedings, it will be necessary for the Family Court to determine the incomes and earning potential of both parties. Sometimes, it becomes important for the Court to know how much each spouse spent throughout the course of the marriage, or some part of it. Canceled bank checks, pay stubs, and copies of income tax returns are useful records for helping the Court determine the answers to these questions. If you can find these records or other records of earnings and expenditures, you should secure them.

Court Actions That Change the Marital Relationship

Overview

Court actions that change the marital relationship are collectively referred to as "marital litigation." Divorces, annulments, and actions for separate support and maintenance are customarily considered to be types of marital litigation. Each of these types of marital litigation is discussed in this section.

There is no cause of action in South Carolina for a "legal separation," although some confusion remains about this. Married couples are not required to go through a court proceeding to obtain permission to live apart. There is no such thing as an "illegal separation." Any married couple who want to live separate and apart may do so without permission from a court. Separating spouses are not required to fill out any paperwork or to receive anyone's permission.

Even when one spouse wants the couple to stay together, but the other spouse refuses to live in the same house, their separation is "legal." However, a spouse who unjustifiably refuses to live with the other spouse may suffer some legal disadvantages during the course of marital litigation, especially if the Family Court concludes that the spouse who refused to continue living as a couple was primarily at fault in causing the breakdown of the marriage.

Some things that happen between spouses during or leading up to divorces could serve as grounds for legal actions that are independent from divorce or other marital litigation. For example, if one spouse steals or destroys property belonging to the other spouse, such misconduct could warrant criminal prosecution and support a lawsuit for damages. Similarly, if one spouse inflicts bodily harm on the other spouse that is sufficient to serve as a ground for divorce in South Carolina, the aggressive spouse's conduct would almost certainly be severe enough to warrant criminal prosecution for domestic abuse or for assault and battery, and it could serve as a basis for a tort lawsuit seeking compensation for injuries and pain and suffering (see the section on violence in Chapter Four).

There are far too many potential legal claims arising from the dissolution of marriages to discuss fully in this book. If you think that your spouse may have engaged in criminal behavior or other misconduct that harmed you or your legal rights, you should consult an attorney and seek advice about your legal rights and the most likely consequences of pursuing legal remedies.

Annulment

An annulment declares that a marriage never existed because of some defect. Annulment actions are rarely brought today because of the extraordinary circumstances required to obtain an annulment and because the availability of no fault divorces makes it possible to get out of any marriage. Before no fault divorces became available in 1969, an annulment action provided the only possible way to get out of a marriage without proving marital misconduct by one spouse.

Defective marriages may be either void or voidable. In a void marriage, the circumstances are such that the marriage could never have come into being. A voidable marriage is recognized under the law as a valid marriage until a court action is brought by one of the parties to prove it invalid.

The following example illustrates the essential differences. Suppose Tom and Mary are parties to a voidable, but not void, marriage and Tom dies. Mary, the surviving spouse, is legally entitled to all legal rights and obligations stemming from the marriage relationship, if there was no court adjudication during the lifetimes of the parties that the marriage was void. After one spouse dies the validity of the marriage cannot be attacked.

A void marriage, by contrast, creates none of the rights and obligations that stem from the marriage relationship. Thus, if Tom and Mary are parties to a void marriage, no court adjudication is required to make it void. It is simply void. A void marriage may be declared void by judicial action at the request of any interested individual at any time, even after the death of one or both spouses.

South Carolina's Family Courts have exclusive jurisdiction over actions for annulment of marriages, that is, the Family Court is the only court in South Carolina that can grant an annulment. Once the Court has jurisdiction of the annulment suit it also has jurisdiction to resolve all other issues presented, including property division, child custody and support, alimony, and attorney's fees. Since an annulment treats the marriage as if it had never existed, it would follow that no alimony could be awarded and no property could be divided since none would have been acquired during a nonexisting marital relationship. However, this approach could impose an unnecessary hardship on one of the parties, especially if they have lived together for a considerable period of time. Consequently, exceptions were created to the basic rule that annulled marriages are to be treated as though they never existed. South Carolina cases have ruled that an exception exists with respect to property division, and it is possible that the appellate courts would rule that the Family Court also has authority to award alimony following an annulment if a Court would award it in a divorce action.

The first question to consider is whether the requirements for establishing either a statutory law marriage or a common law marriage have been met. If not, then the marriage can be annulled. The requirements for establishing valid marriages are discussed in Chapter One.

One ground for obtaining an annulment is lack of cohabitation (living together as husband and wife). If a marriage has not been consummated by the cohabitation of the parties, the Court may declare such contract void for want of consent of either of the contracting parties or for any other reason that proves that the agreement of the parties to be married was not a valid contract. Cohabitation of the parties can probably be established if the parties lived together as husband and wife, even if they did not have sexual relations.

An annulment may be granted, however, even if the parties have cohabited as husband and wife, if the marriage is bigamous (one of the parties was already married) or incestuous (they are related too closely by blood or marriage as provided by state statute). Marriages can also be annulled if the parties never engaged in sexual relations. Many Family Court judges are skeptical, however, about testimony claiming this ground for annulment.

A marriage can also be annulled if one of the parties enters into it under duress. The threats or violence constituting duress, however, must be of such nature as to inspire a great fear of bodily harm in a person of ordinary firmness and it must dominate throughout the transaction to such an extent that the injured party could not and did not act as a free agent.

A marriage procured by certain kinds of fraud can be annulled in South Carolina, unless the marriage has been consummated by cohabitation. However, the fraud must involve matters that constitute the essentials of the marriage relation. Thus, misrepresentations about one party's character, social standing, or fortune are not grounds for an annulment. The misrepresentations that justify an annulment might include fraudulent representations about sanity (but not about being treated for mental illness), impotency, sterility, or an inclination to have children or not to have children contrary to a premarital understanding. Although South Carolina law is not clear about this, some jurisdictions apply a materiality rule, holding that, if the fraud is of such a material nature that the plaintiff would not have entered the marriage but for the fraud, the marriage may be annulled.

Separate Support and Maintenance

Actions for separate support and maintenance are usually filed when one party to the marriage desires to end it, but none of the fault grounds for divorce exist and the parties need help from the Family Court in sorting things out while they wait for one year to pass before seeking a no fault divorce. Separate support and maintenance actions might also be filed by couples who have decided to live separate and apart, but who have not yet made a decision to get a divorce even though legal grounds exist.

Although the term "separate support and maintenance" suggests that a request for spousal support or child support must be made, this is not so. A judge can decide any of the same issues in a separate support and maintenance action as in a divorce case, except that a divorce cannot be granted (if grounds for divorce arise while a separate support and maintenance action is pending, the pleadings can be amended to ask for a divorce, thus converting it into a divorce action). The Court can resolve disputes about child or spousal support, child custody, visitation, or property division. Separate support and maintenance actions are also a vehicle for asking the Family Court to approve agreements that the parties have reached about these matters. There are many reasons for seeking approval of agreements. The parties may want to make sure that their agreements will not be overturned later during a divorce proceeding, or they may not want to wait until a divorce proceeding to be able to sell jointly owned property or to manage businesses in which both parties have an interest.

The Family Court has exclusive jurisdiction to hear and decide actions for separate support and maintenance. No provision in the law explains where an action for separate support and maintenance should be filed. Therefore, you may be able to file an action in any county you choose in South Carolina. However, the safest course of action is to file it in the same locations where you would be allowed to file a divorce action. (Litigants seeking a divorce sometimes have a choice of locations in which they can properly file their pleadings. It can be any county that falls into one of the following categories: (a) the county in which the defendant resides at the time of the commencement of the action, (b) the county in which the plaintiff resides if the defendant is a nonresident or after due diligence cannot be found, or (c) the county in which the parties last resided together as husband and wife unless the plaintiff is a nonresident, in which case it must be brought in the county in which the defendant resides.)

Actions for separate support and maintenance have permanent consequences. They are completely separate legal proceedings from divorce actions, although they may be the preliminary round in litigation leading to divorce. Once a final order is issued in a separate support and maintenance action, matters that are covered by the order cannot be relitigated during a subsequent divorce proceeding.

Similarly, agreements between separated spouses that are approved by the Family Court during actions for separate support and maintenance will be binding in the future. For example, if spousal support (alimony) is requested in the pleadings in a separate support and maintenance action, a court-approved agreement to forego it would bar a subsequent request for spousal support in a divorce action. However, care must be taken to get a ruling by the trial judge on the merits of the issues covered by the agreement if one wants to rely on a separate maintenance and support action as a final disposition of disputed issues. Submitting an agreement for approval without offering any other supporting evidence may not be enough to avoid future litigation.

If requested to do so, the Family Court can order a final division of marital property in an action for separate support and maintenance. This is so although public policy in South Carolina encourages reconciliation and the division of marital property would seem to remove one incentive for separated spouses to attempt a reconciliation and resume marital cohabitation.

Spousal support that is awarded pursuant to an action for separate support and maintenance can be modified for the same reason as spousal support awarded in a divorce action: a material change in circumstances. Of course, it cannot terminate upon remarriage because the parties are not yet divorced and remarriage is impossible. However, spousal support awarded in an action for separate support and maintenance will end if the parties become divorced unless the divorce decree provides for alimony.

Reconciliation terminates any ongoing or prospective obligations created by a separate support and maintenance agreement or order, although it has no effect on any provisions about property division that have been executed already at the time of the reconciliation, for example, changing the titles to the cars or to the marital home.

Divorce

> **In General**

You cannot get a divorce in South Carolina unless you can establish facts that support one of the statutory grounds for divorce. If a ground for divorce exists, you can get a divorce even over the objection of your spouse.

The only form of divorce recognized in South Carolina is divorce *a vinculo matrimonii* (divorce from the bonds of marriage). The overall trend of legislation and judicial decision making has been one toward increasing the ability of spouses to separate and divorce. Although this trend is evident in South Carolina law, South Carolina remains one of the most conservative states with regard to divorce. It is the public policy of South Carolina to foster and protect marriage, to make it a permanent and public institution, to encourage the parties to live together, and to prevent separation.

South Carolina is the only state in which the grounds for divorce are included in its Constitution. The Constitution of 1895 barred divorce, stating simply that "[d]ivorces from the bonds of matrimony shall not be allowed in this State." This remained the law of South Carolina until the Constitution was amended in 1949 to allow divorces on the grounds of adultery, desertion, physical cruelty, or habitual drunkenness. In 1969, the Constitution was amended to allow divorce on the ground of continuous separation without cohabitation for three years. The required period of separation for a no fault divorce was shortened to one year in 1979.

The Family Court has exclusive jurisdiction to hear and determine actions for divorce. Family Courts are located in the courthouses of every county in South Carolina.

Litigants seeking a divorce may have a choice of locations in which they can properly file their pleadings. Actions for divorce from the bonds of matrimony must be tried in the county (a) in which the defendant resides at the time of the commencement of the action, (b) in which the plaintiff resides if the defendant is a nonresident or after due diligence cannot be found, or (c) in which the parties last resided together as husband and wife unless the plaintiff is a nonresident, in which case it must be brought in the county in which the defendant resides. A party wishing to file for divorce may do so in any county that fits one of these categories.

➢ Residency Requirements

You must satisfy one of the requirements for residence before you can file for divorce in South Carolina: (1) you must have resided at least one year in the state prior to the commencement of the action, or (2) if you are a nonresident, your spouse must have resided in the state for one year prior to the commencement of an action, or (3) if both parties are residents of the state, you must have resided in South Carolina at least three months prior to the commencement of an action.

South Carolina does not recognize the validity of divorces obtained by South Carolina residents in other jurisdictions, whether it is another state such as Nevada or another country such as Haiti (two places with short residency requirements). A divorce obtained in another jurisdiction has no force or effect in South Carolina if both parties to the marriage are domiciled in South Carolina when the proceeding for divorce is commenced. This means that people who reside in South Carolina must qualify for a divorce under the laws of South Carolina or remain married.

If a person moves to another jurisdiction and stays there long enough to meet its residency requirements for obtaining a divorce, the divorce might be recognized as a valid divorce by that jurisdiction but not by South Carolina, if the person lives in the other jurisdiction for less than 18 months prior to getting the divorce. South Carolina law states that a person who leaves South Carolina to obtain a divorce but either returns within 18 months or maintains a residence in South Carolina will be regarded as a domiciliary of South Carolina who simply has sought a different and improper forum in which to get a divorce. On the other hand, a person who obtains a divorce decree from some place other than South Carolina then uses it to his or her benefit may not be allowed by the Family Court to deny its validity if it would be detrimental to the other spouse.

➢ Grounds and Proof

● In General

There are only five grounds for divorce in South Carolina: (1) adultery; (2) desertion for a period of one year; (3) physical cruelty; (4) habitual drunkenness, provided, that this ground shall be construed to include habitual drunkenness caused by the use of any narcotic drug; and (5) living separate and apart without cohabitation for a period of one year. Mental cruelty is not a ground for divorce in South Carolina, although it might justify a departure from the marital home.

If a divorce is granted on any ground, it moots the question of whether a divorce should have been granted on any other ground. This means that no one can insist that the Family Court grant a divorce on a particular ground, even when the evidence establishes that more than one ground for divorce exists.

Alimony can be barred on the basis of adultery, irrespective of the ground used as the basis for divorce, but only if the adultery was committed before either: (1) the formal signing of a written property or marital settlement agreement, (2) the entry of a permanent court order of separate maintenance and support, or (3) the entry of a permanent court order approving a property settlement or marital agreement of the parties.

As a technical matter, it makes increasingly less difference whether one uses a fault ground or a no fault ground as the basis for the divorce. To the extent that fault is relevant to issues in dispute between the parties, evidence of the relative misconduct of the parties can be presented to and considered by the Court even where the ground being used for the divorce is the no fault ground based on one year separation. Some attorneys believe, however, that stating fault grounds in the pleadings has an important psychological effect on the opposing party, opposing counsel, and trial judges, which effect may influence decisions about a variety of issues in the case such as child custody and alimony.

The relative fault of the parties is one factor to be considered by the Court in making an equitable division of property award, but it does not justify a severe penalty in making a division of the marital property.

In the final analysis, the decision to use a fault ground (other than adultery which can bar alimony) when the parties have been separated for more than one year may be determined more by the client's interest in making a record of the fact that the divorce was caused by the spouse rather than by consideration of any legal consequences.

- **Living Separate and Apart Without Cohabitation for One Year**

Neither spouse is any more or any less entitled to a no fault divorce than the other. At either party's request, the Court may grant a divorce to one or both parties on the ground of one year separation.

Both parties must be conscious of the fact of the separation before a divorce on the basis of one year separation can be granted, even though it is possible for a separation to take place at the insistence of only one spouse. For example, a divorce on the basis of one year separation will not be granted to one spouse where the other spouse is living separate and apart in a physical sense, but is unaware of the separation because of a commitment to the South Carolina State Hospital as a mental patient.

Similarly, separations caused by military service cannot be used as a basis for divorce. However, if the parties separate before one of them is ordered to move by the military or if the reasons for separating are independent of the military service, the time for establishing the year's separation can continue to run while a spouse is away in military service.

Spouses are not living "separate and apart" for purposes of the divorce statute if they continue to maintain a single household under one roof, even if they can prove that they lived in separate rooms of the marital home and had no sexual relations for more than a year. To allow divorces under such circumstances would encourage collusion between dissatisfied partners of a marriage.

The no fault ground for divorce requires spouses to live separate and apart "without cohabitation" for one year. No explanation of the meaning of "cohabitation" is supplied in the statutory law. Cohabitation has been defined in case law as "living together as man and wife" and as "living together in the same house."

It is not clear whether parties who have sexual relations or who attempt to reconcile during a period of separation are required to wait another full 12 months after the event before they can be divorced. Statutory law does not address the issue, nor does South Carolina appellate case law. No court ruling on the issue should be expected unless it is presented as a secondary issue in an appeal. If a divorce is denied on the basis that one year has not passed since the parties had sexual relations or attempted to reconcile, not many people would be willing to spend the money and effort to appeal that ruling. A new one-year period will very likely have been established by the time an appellate decision would be rendered.

For now, the result of seeking a divorce after a year during which there was some sexual activity between separated spouses will depend on the philosophy of the judge who hears the case. When faced with evidence showing sexual intercourse during the one-year period, some Family Court judges will examine the intentions of the parties and the facts surrounding their sexual intercourse. If the acts of sexual intercourse were casual or recreational, and neither party intended to resume the marriage, they will grant the divorce. Other Family Court judges, however, consistently rule that even an isolated act of sexual relations requires the period of separation to start over. It is possible, but less likely, that some Family Court judges would grant a divorce after an attempted reconciliation of the marriage. Some jurisdictions allow no fault divorces to go forward after failed trial reconciliations. South Carolina appellate courts have not ruled on this issue.

- **Adultery**

Historically, adultery has been one of the most common grounds for divorce. Sexual fidelity is a fundamental duty of the marital relationship. As far as the law is concerned, the contract of marriage is, in its essence, an agreement between a man and a woman to cohabit with each other and with each other only. This means that husbands and wives must confine their sexual activities exclusively to one another. Sexual relations with a person other than the marriage partner are illicit because they violate this marital duty of exclusiveness.

Adultery is defined as the act of having sexual intercourse with someone other than one's spouse. Adultery does not require the normal act of consummation between a man and a woman, however. South Carolina law does not specifically define the sex acts that constitute adultery, but the appellate courts have held that proof of "sexual intimacy" is enough to support a finding of adultery. Also, a divorce can be granted in South Carolina on the ground of adultery where one spouse is involved in a homosexual relationship.

Proof of adultery must be clear and positive, and the infidelity must be established by a clear preponderance of the evidence, that is, enough evidence to convince a Family Court judge that adultery actually occurred. Proof of adultery may be by circumstantial evidence, and proof of "opportunity and inclination" to commit adultery is sufficient to sustain a finding of adultery. This is because adultery by its very nature is an activity that takes place in private. Indeed, if it were not for circumstantial evidence, the practice of adultery would scarcely be known to exist.

A finding of adultery is allowed where there is evidence of both the opportunity to commit adultery and the inclination to commit adultery. Simply proving that a spouse and an alleged paramour were in the same place where they might have committed adultery, without more, will not support a finding of adultery. For instance, proving that they both stayed in the same hotel is not sufficient, whereas proving that they slept in the same bed may be. Simply proving that a man and a woman were together may establish that they had an opportunity to commit adultery, but it does not establish that they were inclined to do so. It is probably necessary to produce some evidence of a romantic interest or sexual relationship to obtain a divorce based on adultery. This may include evidence that they were holding hands, kissing, or engaging in other conduct that would lead a reasonable observer to conclude that they were romantically involved.

The Family Court is allowed, however, to infer state of mind from the circumstances. The same evidence that proves the opportunity can also prove the disposition. For example, if a man and a woman are seen going into a motel room late at night and not coming out until the next morning, it can be inferred that they committed adultery. Unless something to the contrary appears, no other evidence is required to warrant a finding of adultery.

There is some question about the degree of specificity that is required to sustain a finding of adultery. One case held that the proof must be sufficiently definite to identify the time and place of the offense and the circumstances under which it was committed, but the more accepted rule seems to be that approximate times, places, and circumstances are sufficient to prove adultery. Common sense often dictates a judge's determination of whether or not adultery occurred. The key is whether the judge is fully convinced that adultery was committed and the alleged adulterer had a fair opportunity to defend or refute the charge.

Since the sexual intercourse involved must be "voluntary," it is generally held that an element of adultery is a guilty intent. In other words, the person engaging in adultery must know that he or she is doing so. It follows that a substantial mistake of fact, or an incapacity on the part of the accused, will serve to prevent a finding of adultery. Thus, it has been said that it is not adultery where the wife has intercourse with a man not her husband through mistake, she believing him to be her husband in the dark. It is likely, however, that South Carolina courts would rule that intercourse brought on by self-induced intoxication or drug use will not be shielded from designation as adulterous, since an intoxicated person is generally held to have entered that state voluntarily. While South Carolina allows the defense of mental illness as an excuse for adultery, the person raising this defense must prove that at the time the adultery was committed, she or he was unable to appreciate the wrongfulness of the conduct due to mental illness.

A South Carolina statute about 100 years old makes adultery a crime punishable by a fine of from $100 to $500, or imprisonment for from six months to one year, or both. The statute defines adultery as "the living together and carnal intercourse with each other or habitual carnal intercourse with each other without living together of a man and woman when either is lawfully married to some other person." Prosecutions for the crime of adultery are almost never undertaken, but the crime remains part of the statutory law, and the Solicitor for each judicial circuit has the discretion to decide whether to prosecute someone for committing adultery.

For many years, spouses accused of adultery and their alleged paramours tried to use the criminal law against adultery as a shield. They would refuse to answer questions about adultery on the basis that answering such questions would violate their right against self-incrimination as guaranteed by the Fifth Amendment of the United States Constitution. This risk exists because statements made by a person in a civil case can be used against the person in a criminal prosecution. The spouse trying to prove adultery would counter this tactic by obtaining a grant of immunity from criminal prosecution from the Solicitor's office.

Case law now allows a Family Court judge to draw an adverse inference against a witness who is accused of committing adultery if the witness asserts the Fifth Amendment privilege against self-incrimination and refuses to answer questions about the alleged adultery after being granted immunity from prosecution for criminal adultery. If immunity from criminal prosecution has been granted, a Family Court judge may even be able to order the witness to answer questions about the alleged adultery. It appears likely that the Family Court can draw a negative inference even if immunity has not been granted, especially if the party raising the self-incrimination shield is seeking affirmative relief of some sort from the Family Court. For example, a person asserting the Fifth Amendment in refusing to answer questions about alleged adultery may forfeit the right to seek alimony. This is an area of developing law in South Carolina.

● **Desertion**

Desertion was once the most common ground upon which divorces were granted in South Carolina. Today, desertion is rarely used as the basis for granting a divorce because it is much easier to establish a no fault ground based on one-year separation. A no fault divorce can be proved more easily than desertion, and the courts will consider the same factors in deciding any disputed issues, irrespective of the basis on which the divorce is being sought. If one party deserves better treatment from the Court because the other spouse is a deserter, such misconduct and any advantage to be derived from it can be presented to and considered by the Court in a no fault divorce, if it is relevant to issues before the Court. Thus, the information presented in this section is largely of academic, not practical, interest. However, it may be of some use in those cases in which there is an advantage to be gained in negotiations or personal satisfaction by labeling someone as a deserter, or when one believes that alleging desertion will have a positive psychological effect on the trial judge.

The essential elements of desertion are:

(1)   cessation from cohabitation for one year,

(2)   intent of the absenting party not to resume cohabitation,

(3)   absence of consent, and

(4)   absence of justification for the cessation.

The cessation from cohabitation must persist for a full year. The time period is measured from the date of initial desertion to the time of filing. An actual physical departure is required. A refusal to engage in sexual relations for a year, without a physical departure, does not constitute desertion inasmuch as "cohabitation" connotes more than physical intimacy. Locking a spouse out of the marital home will probably constitute desertion, absent a good justification for doing so.

If the deserting spouse returns or makes a good faith offer to return, the desertion ground is lost. Furthermore, a refusal by the deserted spouse to accept a good faith reconciliation offer could create a desertion ground in favor of the original deserter. If a party to a mutual agreement to separate has a change of heart and offers to reconcile and the other party refuses, the refusing party becomes a deserter and the other party could seek a divorce on that ground a year from the date of the refusal. A refusal to accept a reconciliation offer will not make one a deserter, however, if the offer is insufficient. Such an offer must be made in good faith and must ordinarily be made before the cause of action accrues, that is, before the end of the one-year period following the desertion. "Good faith" is a matter of fact, and its existence is determined from an examination of all surrounding circumstances.

The desertion ground is lost if the abandoned spouse agrees to the separation during the year or manifests an unwillingness to have the departed spouse return. However, the mere silence of an abandoned spouse is probably not consent to the desertion. This is the nearly universal rule.

Not all departures from the marital abode are sufficient to give rise to a cause of action for divorce, even though they are intentional and the remaining spouse does not consent to the departure. Conduct on the part of the remaining party may justify the departing spouse's action. For example, a spouse's failure to work and provide the necessities of life for the other spouse may justify a departure from the marital home. A failure to provide reasonable living conditions could be sufficient justification to leave a spouse. Making life intolerable for a spouse might justify the departure of that spouse even if the new misconduct is not sufficient to support a fault ground for divorce.

- **Physical Cruelty**

Some sort of physical violence is required to give rise to a cause of action for a divorce on the ground of physical cruelty. The nature of conduct that will give rise to a cause of action as physical cruelty is defined in South Carolina as "actual personal violence, or such a course of physical treatment as endangers life, limb, or health, and renders cohabitation unsafe." Continued acts of personal violence producing physical pain or bodily injury and a fear of future danger are recognized as sufficient cause for a divorce for cruelty in nearly all jurisdictions, especially where accompanied by other acts of ill treatment. It is not every slight violence, however, committed by the husband or wife against the other, even in anger, that will authorize the divorce.

It is generally held that a single act of physical cruelty does not ordinarily constitute a ground for divorce, unless it is so severe and atrocious as to endanger life, or unless the act indicates an intention to do serious bodily harm or causes reasonable apprehension of serious danger in the future. Although "slight violence" ordinarily does not constitute physical cruelty, the appellate courts have held that a single episode of violence may warrant a divorce in some instances. A single assault by one spouse upon the other spouse can constitute physical cruelty, if the assault is life-threatening, indicates an intention to do serious bodily harm, or is of such a degree as to raise a reasonable apprehension of great bodily harm in the future. For example, in one case a wife fired 16 shots through the bedroom door with her husband on the other side. Although none of the shots hit the husband, the Court felt that a divorce on the ground of physical cruelty was warranted even though it was a single incident.

Refusing to have sex with your spouse does not constitute physical cruelty, even where it is alleged that the denial threatens the mental health of the plaintiff. Also, a nagging wife is not physical cruelty, even if it prevents sleep.

Mental cruelty and verbal abuse are not grounds for divorce in South Carolina.

• Habitual Drunkenness and Drug Abuse

The ground of habitual drunkenness includes habitual drunkenness caused not only by alcohol but also by the use of a narcotic drug. In order to prove habitual drunkenness, there must be a showing that the abuse of alcohol caused the breakdown of the marriage and that such abuse existed at or near the time of filing for divorce. It is not clear how near the time of filing for divorce the drunkenness must continue.

There is no clear definition of "habitual drunkenness." One definition is "the fixed habit of frequently getting drunk; but it does not necessarily imply continual drunkenness." However, neither statutory nor case law defines "fixed habit," "frequently," or "drunk." In one appellate case, the wife's treatment for alcoholism three months before the husband filed for divorce was enough to get a divorce. One need not be an alcoholic, however, to support a finding of habitual drunkenness. The courts will consider the amount of alcohol being consumed and its effect, as well as the frequency of imbibing. It is sufficient that the use or abuse of alcohol or drugs is "habitual" and causes the breakdown of normal marital relations.

➤ Defenses Not Related to Proof of the Grounds for Divorce

There are many defenses to divorce actions that are not related to whether a ground for divorce can be proven. Some of them are rarely used today. They are discussed below in the following order: collusion, connivance, recrimination, condonation, reconciliation, and provocation.

● Collusion

If the parties to a divorce engage in conduct solely for the purpose of obtaining a divorce, the Family Court will deny the divorce for the reason that it is collusive and it would allow a person to succeed in perpetrating a fraud on the Court to grant the divorce. A South Carolina statute says that "[i]f it shall appear to the satisfaction of the Court that the parties to any divorce proceeding colluded or that the act complained of was done with the knowledge or assent of the plaintiff for the purpose of obtaining a divorce the court shall not grant such divorce."

South Carolina has not defined collusion in the context of marital litigation. However, collusion was defined in a case involving insurance fraud as "fraud which, in judicial proceedings, is a secret agreement between two persons that one should institute suit against the other in order to obtain the decision of a judicial tribunal for some sinister purpose, or on perjured testimony." Another state defined collusion in the context of divorce as "an agreement between a husband and wife that one of them shall commit, or appear to have committed, or to be represented in court as having committed, acts constituting a cause of divorce, for the purpose of enabling the other to obtain a divorce."

Note that there are two principal facets to the above: first, that there must be an agreement between the spouses; second, that the agreement must have to do with the substance of the act or acts alleged to be the ground for divorce.

- **Connivance**

The defense of connivance probably exists in South Carolina. Connivance in the law of divorce exists when the evidence shows that the spouse who is complaining about the other spouse's conduct consented, expressly or impliedly, to the misconduct. For example, a husband would be able to prevent a divorce based on his adultery if he could prove that his wife hired a prostitute to seduce him. A corrupt intent on the part of the person seeking the divorce that the party at fault should engage in misconduct is an essential element of connivance. If the consent was actively given, the intent is impliedly corrupt and the defense is complete.

The defense has certain similarities to that of collusion. The most obvious distinction lies in the fact that only one spouse needs to be planning for or agreeing to the commission of the marital offense to establish connivance, while collusion requires that both participants have ill motives. Additionally, the presentation of a collusive divorce may involve fabrication of the entire marital offense. The presentation of a divorce wherein connivance is a reasonable defense will necessarily involve the actual commission of a marital wrong. To an extent, both defenses come about as a result of the state's obligation to keep its court system free from mistaken decisions and to prevent the misleading of judicial officers.

From the perspective of the effect of the defense on marital litigants, it is less easy to see the justification. Presumably if one spouse is willing to commit a marital offense and the other is willing to consent to it or arrange for it, there is not much left in the marriage to preserve. However, it is possible that a scheming spouse could arrange a situation in which the other spouse would succumb to temptation even though that spouse was genuinely desirous of maintaining the marriage relation. To the extent that the law of divorce is supposed to continue to contain an element of punishment for spouses who are "guilty," it makes sense to maintain the defense of connivance.

• Recrimination

The recrimination defense is raised when both parties have engaged in marital misconduct that would serve as grounds for divorce, but one of the parties does not want to be divorced. If a party raises the defense of recrimination, the Family Court will not grant a divorce if it is proven that both parties have a fault ground for divorce. (Recrimination is not a defense to an action for divorce based upon one year's separation.) Thus, if both parties prove the other committed adultery and one of them raises the defense of recrimination, no divorce will be granted, unless they lived separate and apart for over a year prior to the filing of the pleadings. The marital offense does not have to be of the same nature. For example, if one party is seeking a divorce based on physical cruelty, but the party seeking the divorce has committed adultery, the recrimination defense could block the divorce if the defendant raises it.

• Condonation

Condonation is one of the most important defenses in South Carolina marital litigation. Proof of condonation will defeat a divorce action brought on a fault ground.

The basic elements needed to establish the defense of condonation are forgiveness, a mutual intention to renew the full marital relationship, usually cohabitation, and actual knowledge of the marital offense. Condonation in the law of divorce means forgiveness, express or implied, by one spouse for a breach of marital duty by the other. More specifically, it is the forgiveness of an antecedent matrimonial offense on condition that it shall not be repeated, and that the offender shall thereafter treat the forgiving party with conjugal kindness.

Condonation may be expressly stated or inferred from conduct. For example, condonation can be implied by continuing to cohabit with a misbehaving spouse after learning of the misconduct. Continued cohabitation for a considerable period of time is conclusive proof of condonation.

Proof of ongoing sexual relations may establish condonation, however, proof of one act of intercourse without more would probably not suffice to establish condonation. Conversely, condonation can be proved without specifically proving a resumption of sexual relations.

Condonation is not a valid defense unless the supposed condoner has actual knowledge of the marital offense that he or she is allegedly condoning, and not merely a suspicion that the marital offense has occurred. A presumption that a spouse has knowledge of the marital misconduct of the other spouse can be created by the passage of time, that is, the courts will assume knowledge of marital misconduct that occurred a long time ago.

Condonation is a conditional forgiveness, the implied condition being that the guilty party shall in the future refrain from committing any matrimonial offense. Subsequent marital misconduct may revive the condoned conduct as a viable ground for divorce. For example, if a spouse condones conduct that otherwise would provide a basis for a divorce on the ground of physical cruelty, no divorce can be brought based on the condoned conduct. However, the facts of the earlier misconduct could be used to obtain a divorce if the forgiven spouse later engages in conduct, such as physical violence that is not quite of a degree sufficient to obtain a divorce on physical cruelty, if such conduct reasonably leads the forgiving spouse to fear that the physical cruelty will be repeated.

● Reconciliation

Reconciliation is similar to condonation. The major difference is that it does not necessarily involve the forgiveness of marital misconduct, e.g., reconciliation may occur following a period of separation that was prompted by a mutual feeling by spouses that they no longer loved each other. Another difference is that reconciliation is associated with ending a period of physical separation while condonation may occur while spouses are continuing to live together. "Reconciliation" has been defined as "resumption of marital cohabitation in its fullest sense, with the husband and wife resuming their status, positions, services, privileges and duties as marital partners in all material respects. Reconciliation is a matter of mutual intent to resume married life entirely."

The most significant difference between reconciliation and condonation is that condonation is always conditional (the antecedent matrimonial offense is forgiven on condition that it shall not be repeated) whereas a true reconciliation is unconditional. It is often difficult to tell the difference. Another distinction is that condonation always involves the forgiveness of some sort of misconduct, whereas reconciliation may follow a period of separation that was not brought about by misconduct.

● Provocation

The provocation defense is essentially "yes, I did it, but I would not have done it but for his (or her) provocation." When raised, it is usually in the context of physical cruelty allegations. However, the defense is not often used, in large part because South Carolina courts have not accepted the defense if the retaliatory conduct is disproportionate to the conduct alleged to have provoked it. If the provoking acts and the retaliatory acts are similarly violent and amount to mutual combat, it appears that the defense of provocation will be allowed and no divorce will be granted in South Carolina, even if it means that two people who appear capable of and interested in harming each other are forced to remain married.

> ## Consequences of Divorce[4]

Divorce ends the marriage, but it does not affect all of the legal rights and obligations created by the marriage.

● Interpersonal Rights and Obligations

If a divorced couple wishes to continue living together, there is nothing to stop them from doing so other than their personal values.

Divorce removes the legal right and social expectation that married couples will engage in sexual intercourse. Although it is no longer viewed by many people as a serious threat of criminal prosecution, it remains the law in South Carolina that people who live together and engage in carnal intercourse without being married are committing the crime of fornication.

Divorce ends the statutorily imposed obligation of spouses to provide support for each other. The only support obligations between former spouses are any that might have been imposed by the Family Court in its divorce decree.

A divorced person can choose to continue using the surname used during the marriage or any other name he or she desires. South Carolina appears to continue to recognize the common law rule that

---

[4] This section should be read together with the section on "Consequences of Marriage" in Chapter One.

"a man may lawfully change his name, or by general usage or habit acquire another name than that originally borne by him, without the intervention of Court or Legislature."

Those people who want some proof that they have legally changed their names can ask the Family Court to issue an order allowing them to change their names, as long as it is not for the purpose of defrauding creditors or others. The Family Court is specifically authorized upon the granting of final judgment of divorce to allow a wife to resume using her maiden name or the name of any former husband. The Family Court is also authorized to let a divorced person use a different name than specifically designated by statute and to grant a request for a name change independent of divorce actions (perhaps, even before a person files for divorce).

- **Assets and Liabilities**

Divorce for the most part has no effect on the property rights of either party, unless one or both spouses seek intervention by the Family Court. However, divorce automatically severs any joint tenancy in real estate held by a husband and wife with no other tenants and vests the interests in both parties as tenants in common, unless otherwise provided by a court. Neither party continues to acquire any interest in the assets of the other once they are divorced.

The "doctrine of necessaries" does not apply to divorced people. However, the duty to provide "necessaries" to a spouse continues during the pendency of a suit for divorce, even if the spouse does not request temporary alimony.

Perhaps the most significant consequence of divorce is that divorced persons lose their right to inherit anything from each other, unless part of the estate is left to the surviving spouse in a will prepared after the divorce. Divorce revokes any disposition of property to a spouse under a will, any provision conferring on the spouse a power of appointment, and any nomination of the spouse as executor, trustee, conservator, or guardian, unless the will specifically states that such matters will survive a divorce. Other portions of the will remain valid following a divorce, unless the will provides otherwise.

- **Children**

Divorce does not affect the legitimacy of children.

Divorce has no legal effect on the obligations of parents for the welfare, education, and care of their children.

The Family Court is authorized to change the last names of children following divorce, if it determines that it would be in their best interests.

CHAPTER THREE

------◆------

How Cases Proceed
Through the Family Court

(Actions for Separate Support and Maintenance,
Annulments, and Divorces)

Introduction

This chapter provides an overview of the steps involved with
processing marital litigation through the Family Court. Everyone who
wants a divorce must eventually go through the Family Court process.
No divorce can be granted in South Carolina without first having a
hearing before a Family Court judge and obtaining from the judge a
written order granting a divorce.

The Family Court is an "equity" court. That is, the goal of
Family Court judges is to accomplish the fairest results possible,
within the guidelines set by law. Nevertheless, litigation in the Family
Court is an adversarial process with each side seeking to achieve
certain objectives. The adversarial system works best when both sides
are represented by qualified lawyers who can organize the issues in a
case, present evidence, question witnesses, and make arguments to the
trial judge. Judges do not conduct independent investigations of the
facts of each case, therefore, a judge's ability to make the fairest
decision possible is hindered when neither party is represented by a
lawyer or when one party is represented but the other is not.

Most people settle all matters by agreement, usually with the assistance of their lawyers, leaving nothing for the Family Court judge to do other than to decide whether the agreement is fair and whether sufficient evidence has been presented to grant the divorce or annulment. Some people settle everything before filing any pleadings with the Court, while many others settle matters while litigation is pending. When settlements are reached during litigation, the Family Court judge is commonly asked to approve the terms of the settlement and to incorporate them into the final order. Approval by the Family Court improves the probability that the agreement can be enforced if one party does not fully comply with its terms after the divorce.

Most of the final divorce hearings in the Family Court last about 15 minutes because all issues have been settled by agreement. Contested trials, however, can last several hours, several days, or in rare instances even longer.

When the parties are able to settle all matters by agreement before they file any pleadings in court and the ground for divorce is not contested, some of the steps described in this chapter will be skipped and the litigation will proceed to a conclusion much faster. The length of time and the amount of money it takes to process a case through the Family Court is directly related to the ability of the parties to reach agreements about the decisions they face in dissolving their marriage.

Some complex divorce cases can take more than a year to process from the filing of the complaint to the final hearing, but most do not take that long. Once a case is filed in the Family Court, a written request for a final hearing must be delivered to the Family Court Clerk's Office within 12 months (365 days) from the time the complaint is filed, or the case will be stricken from the docket. The purpose of this rule is to encourage parties, attorneys, and judges to expedite the processing of marital litigation as much as possible.

Twelve months is long enough to process most marital litigation cases, but litigants should avoid unnecessarily causing delays and keep an eye on the calendar.

If a case is stricken from the docket, the plaintiff must start the process all over, unless the chief administrative judge of the Family Court for that judicial circuit decides there was good cause for the delay and reinstates the case. An administrative order of the Supreme Court of South Carolina provides that all temporary orders issued in stricken cases will be null and void, but any final orders, e.g., for contempt of court, will remain valid.

This chapter does not provide enough information for litigants to try to handle their own divorces, even those in which full agreement exists between the parties. Its only purpose is to give litigants in the Family Court a better understanding of the stages that their cases will pass through from beginning to end.

Instructions and forms for processing simple divorces have been approved by the South Carolina Supreme Court. "Self-represented litigant divorce packets" are available for free at http://www.sccourts.org/forms/indexSRLdivorcepacket.cfm. The forms are intended for use by people: (1) who have no marital property or marital debts or have reached an agreement on how to divide their property and debts; and (2) who have no children and expect none or have minor children and have reached an agreement as to custody and visitation as well as an amount of child support that meets the minimum requirements set by the South Carolina Child Support Guidelines.

Getting Started

Develop a Game Plan

Unless your situation involves an emergency that must be addressed immediately, you and your lawyer should develop a "game plan" for the litigation before you take any action. You should set goals together and discuss how they can best be accomplished. Your lawyer should help you understand how the lawyer expects the case to proceed and what your role will be at each stage. Your lawyer should tell you what to expect next and when to expect it to happen. You should discuss whether there are tasks that you can undertake, such as gathering and organizing documents. You should review the "game plan" with your lawyer and consider whether it needs to be modified periodically during the litigation, especially after any significant developments such as the receipt of new pleadings from your spouse or any court hearings.

It is your responsibility to make it clear to your lawyer what you want to happen and to help the lawyer understand your priorities. Your lawyer is required by the rules of professional ethics to let you set the objectives of litigation, but your lawyer is also prohibited from helping you pursue improper objectives. You have the right to decide whether to accept or reject any settlement offers.

It is your lawyer's job to tell you if your goals are realistic and, if they are, to help you achieve them. The lawyer should also help you identify alternative ways that your goals might be accomplished and to help you understand the most likely consequences of each course of action. The means by which your goals are pursued are generally within the discretion of the lawyer, but the lawyer should explain to you what the lawyer intends to do and how it will be done – and should give you an opportunity to object to these plans, if you think there is a better way to proceed.

It is not unusual for a person in marital litigation to change his or her mind more than once about objectives and priorities. Divorce is a stressful event for most people, and it is often difficult to make the best decisions possible. Attitudes sometimes change as new events occur and time passes, and people involved in marital litigation frequently reconsider their goals and priorities once they have time to reflect. Unlike most other kinds of litigation where the focus is on a historical event, such as a car crash, marital litigation is complicated by the reality that the relevant facts are not locked in time when litigation is filed. Things continue to happen in people's lives during marital litigation that cause them to change their minds – sometimes because new events may affect how a judge will decide disputed issues.

If you change your mind about what you want to achieve in your case or how you want the lawyer to proceed, communicate this to the lawyer as soon as possible. Also inform the lawyer of any significant new developments in your life (you should ask your lawyer to tell you what kinds of things you should inform the lawyer about). Of course, it can be frustrating to a lawyer when a client changes his or her mind or something happens that could affect the outcome of litigation, but lawyers who practice family law are used to it. Don't be embarrassed to communicate new information to your lawyer. Your lawyer needs to know.

Pleadings

All litigation in South Carolina begins with the filing and service of a summons and complaint (these and any other documents that request the Family Court to do something are collectively referred to as the pleadings). A summons is a short document that simply informs the defendant that an answer to the complaint must be served within 30 days and where it is to be served.

The complaint is the most important document in marital litigation, except for the final order. It names the plaintiff (the person who is asking the Family Court to do something) and the defendant, it provides basic information about the parties and their marriage, it explains what issues are in dispute between the parties, it sets forth the plaintiff's version of the facts, and it tells the Family Court what the plaintiff wants it to do, for example, to grant a divorce, order the defendant to pay child support, or to divide the parties' jointly owned property. The Family Court does not have the authority to take any action other than what it is requested to do by either the plaintiff or defendant in the pleadings.

Marital litigation begins when the summons and complaint are filed with the Clerk of the Family Court. Then, after being assigned a docket number they are served on the defendant. This procedure is different from that in other civil actions where the pleadings are first served, then filed. The pleadings must be accompanied by a cover form obtained from the Clerk that provides basic information about the case. A filing fee is normally required before the Clerk will file the pleadings. This fee can be waived, however, for people who cannot afford to pay the fee. A completed Financial Declaration form should accompany a request for a fee waiver.

Once the Clerk has processed the pleadings and assigned a docket number to the case, the summons and complaint must be served on the defendant. Serving the papers is a very important step in the litigation process. If it is not done correctly, the entire case can be thrown out of court months later. The Family Court is required to ensure that the defendant is given fair notice of the case and the issues in it. If service is not properly accomplished the Family Court does not have jurisdiction to hear the case.

There are several ways to serve the summons and complaint. The pleadings can be served by having a deputy sheriff or someone at least 18 years old who is not an attorney or a party to the action deliver the pleadings to the defendant in person. Alternatively, the defendant can accept service or the plaintiff can mail the pleadings to the defendant by certified mail with restricted delivery and return receipt requested. If done properly, all of these are valid methods for serving papers. Whatever method of service is used, the plaintiff is required to have written evidence that the pleadings were properly served and to file this evidence promptly with the Clerk of the Family Court.

The defendant's response to the complaint is called an answer. This document is where the defendant tells the other side of the story, if there is one, and lets the Family Court and the opposing party know whether there are any issues in dispute and what the defendant wants the Family Court to do about them. The answer should state whether the defendant admits or denies the accuracy of each of the facts stated in the complaint, paragraph by paragraph, line by line.

Sometimes a defendant will want the Family Court to grant some affirmative relief to the defendant. For example, a defendant may ask the Family Court to refuse to grant the plaintiff's request for a divorce on the ground of adultery. This would be part of the answer. The defendant, however, may also ask the Family Court to grant a divorce to the defendant or to decide some issues that were not raised by the plaintiff. Such requests for affirmative relief are called counterclaims. Counterclaims are raised in the same document as the answer and the combined document would be referred to as an answer and counterclaim. If counterclaims are not submitted within 30 days after service of the summons and complaint, the Family Court may not let you raise them at a later time.

On the other hand, Family Court judges will usually allow complaints and answers to be amended if new information comes to light while the case is pending. For example, if the plaintiff files for divorce on the ground of habitual drunkenness, then learns that the defendant committed adultery, the plaintiff would be allowed by most judges to amend the complaint to allege adultery, which if proven would prevent alimony from being awarded.

If counterclaims are included with the answer, the plaintiff has the right to file additional pleadings to respond to them. Similarly, if a complaint or a counterclaim is amended at some point during the litigation, the other party will be given an opportunity to respond to any new allegations.

Even if the defendant does not file an answer, the defendant still has the right to receive notice of the time and date of the final hearing, and the defendant can attend the hearing and give testimony on issues of custody, visitation, alimony, support, equitable distribution of property, and attorneys fees and costs. This is different from other types of litigation in which the plaintiff is deemed entitled to the relief requested in the complaint if the defendant defaults by not serving an answer in a timely manner.

Financial Declarations

The Family Court Rules require both spouses to prepare a Financial Declaration form (available from your lawyer or from the Clerk of the Family Court in each county). This document requires you to set forth your monthly income and expenses in some detail and to list all of the property that is jointly owned by you and your spouse, including debts. This can be a difficult document to fill out, in part because the expenses of people going through divorces may change several times during the divorce process. A lawyer can help you understand how to fill out the Financial Declaration form.

Financial Declaration forms for both parties must be filed with the Clerk of the Family Court and served on the opposing party no later than the first hearing in the case (usually the hearing on motions for temporary relief) or no later than 45 days after the complaint is served, whichever comes first.

There is a natural tendency for people who are involved in divorce proceedings to want to understate their income and assets and to overstate their expenses and debts on the Financial Declaration form. It is extremely important to resist any urge to misstate information on this form. If issues involving the Financial Declaration form become matters of dispute in the divorce, it may be relatively easy to prove that someone has misstated information.

The Financial Declaration form is signed under oath. Therefore, any intentional misstatements of information in it could be considered contempt of court which carries the potential for jail or a fine. More significantly, it gives the other side an opportunity to prove to the Court that you are willing to lie under oath. If this happens, you lose credibility with the trial judge on every other issue about which you need to testify. The Financial Declaration form should be filled out as carefully and accurately as possible.

Temporary Hearings

Temporary hearings (also referred to as *pendente lite* hearings) are very important events in marital litigation. If the parties cannot agree about something and one of the parties asks for temporary relief, a temporary hearing will be held usually within four weeks after the complaint is filed. At this hearing, a Family Court judge will decide how things will be until the final hearing. This can include temporary rulings about child custody and support, use of property, responsibility for debts, spousal support, attorneys' fees, restraining orders, and more.

Although the Family Court judge who conducts the final hearing is not bound by the rulings of the judge at the temporary hearing, the rulings at a temporary hearing can have a significant impact on the outcome of the case. For example, if the judge awards temporary custody of the children to the father, this gives the father an opportunity to establish a record of successful single parenting during the interim between the temporary and final hearings. This can influence the judge who makes the final decision about custody. Temporary hearings should be approached very seriously. Anyone who is facing a temporary hearing is strongly encouraged to seek help from a lawyer.

Requests for temporary hearings are usually filed at the same time as the complaint or answer. This is one of the reasons why pleadings are filed with the Family Court Clerk before being served. If the complaint includes a motion for a temporary hearing, the Clerk will assign a time for the hearing when the case is filed. Therefore, when the complaint is served on the defendant, it will include notice that a temporary hearing is scheduled. This allows temporary hearings to be held fairly quickly after pleadings are filed. This can be very important when people are having trouble resolving their differences without judicial intervention. Unless there is an emergency, the defendant is usually entitled to five days notice of a temporary hearing.

Written affidavits (notarized statements) take the place of live testimony at temporary hearings. They come from anyone who has something relevant to say about the issues. For example, if child custody is contested, affidavits in addition to the parties' own affidavits may be submitted from family members, teachers, doctors, counselors, coaches, Sunday School teachers, ministers or priests, neighbors, parents of the children's friends, and anyone else with information or an opinion about the suitability or unsuitability of either parent to have custody that would seem relevant to the judge.

Lawyers will help clients and witnesses prepare the affidavits, but they can only contain information that the client or witnesses know to be true or at least have a reason to believe to be true. Most lawyers recommend that the affidavits should be written from a first hand perspective, that is, if read aloud, they would sound like the person is speaking directly to the judge. Clients and witnesses who are willing to provide affidavits are sometimes instructed by lawyers to "write from the heart."

A "Background Information Sheet" (SCCA Form 459) must be submitted by each party at the temporary hearing (http://sccourts.org/forms/word/scca459.dot).

Temporary hearings are generally very brief affairs. Most hearings are limited to 15 minutes. It is common for lawyers and clients to work out an agreement before the hearing. If this happens, the lawyers will simply report the terms of the agreement to the judge, who will usually summarily approve the agreement. If one or both parties is not represented by a lawyer, the judge may ask a few questions to establish that both parties understand the agreement and were not coerced into making it.

If there are any disputed issues for the judge to decide, the judge will usually not allow anyone to testify or allow the admission of any evidence other than the pleadings, financial declarations, and no more than eight pages of affidavits submitted by each side. The judge will read the documents and will usually allow the parties' attorneys to make brief arguments before ruling on whatever issues are presented. The judge will usually announce his or her rulings in the courtroom.

Preparing for Settlement or Trial

Discovery

After the pleadings have been filed and the parties know which issues they agree and disagree about, it is often necessary to obtain more information about the disputed issues before a reasonable settlement can be reached. Fundamentally, discovery is an effort by both sides to acquire relevant information from each other so that all parties can better evaluate how a Family Court judge would probably rule on disputed issues. Once enough information has been shared, the lawyers for both parties will frequently make the same predictions about the probable outcome of a trial. This makes it possible for clients to make rational decisions about whether to settle disputed issues or take them to trial.

People involved in marital litigation are encouraged to exchange information and documents voluntarily. Formal discovery is not allowed in the Family Court unless a Family Court judge grants permission to engage in discovery or the parties agree to it in writing or in their pleadings. This policy is intended to speed up the litigation, encourage cooperation, and reduce the costs to the parties. Formal discovery can become very expensive. When it becomes necessary to request permission to use formal discovery, it is usually done by consent of both sides, but even if the request is opposed, the Family Court usually permits it.

The most common kinds of formal discovery in marital litigation are requesting the production of documents and submitting written questions (called interrogatories) to each other. Taking the depositions of the opposing party and other key witnesses is also available, but more expensive. A deposition is a meeting where the lawyer for one side asks questions that a witness for the other side is required to answer under oath. The questions and answers are recorded by a court reporter. No judge is present, and depositions are usually conducted at the offices of the lawyer who is taking the depositions. Taking depositions enables lawyers to evaluate the credibility and character of the people whose depositions are taken and to follow up on information as it arises from the witness' answers. Answers to interrogatories and depositions inform both sides about the likely content of the witness's testimony at trial. This information helps lawyers evaluate the probable outcomes of trials and to counsel their clients accordingly. These discovery techniques also establish a sworn record of the witnesses' stories that can be used to challenge the credibility of witnesses if they say something different during a subsequent court hearing.

Mediation

The traditional way to resolve disputes during marital litigation is for the lawyers to try to negotiate a settlement and to submit any unsettled issues to a Family Court judge for a final ruling. Sometimes this does not produce positive results.

One alternative method of dispute resolution (ADR) is mediation. Mediation gives both parties an opportunity to sit down with a neutral person called a mediator and try to work out an agreement. The idea behind mediation is that most people will be happier with agreements they make themselves than they would be with solutions that are imposed on them by a court. Mediation proponents also believe that most litigants are more capable than a judge of making the best decisions about certain issues, especially custody and visitation of their children.

Mediation is required in all Family Court cases in which any issue is in dispute. The mediation process must be completed before a final hearing can be scheduled. If there are unresolved issues about child custody or visitation, an early mediation of these issues is required.

The parties may select a mediator, or one will be appointed by the Family Court. The mediator is paid by the parties who normally will split the cost.

The Chief Administrative Judge of the Family Court may exempt a case from mediation for good cause. Good cause could be the incapacity of a party (mental or physical illness), incarceration, spousal abuse, substance abuse, child abuse, or a prior attempt at voluntary mediation with a certified mediator.

The mediator will set the schedule for conferences and may recess a conference at any time and set times for reconvening. The mediator, the parties, and their lawyers are required to attend the mediation settlement conference. The parties must participate in at least three hours of mediation unless an agreement is reached sooner. If an agreement is reached, the mediator will provide a Memorandum of Agreement to the parties' attorneys and any guardians *ad litem*. It is the obligation of the parties to seek approval of the agreement by the Family Court.

If a party fails to attend a scheduled mediation conference without good cause, the Court may impose sanctions, including contempt of court (potential fine and jail time), payment of attorneys' fees, mediator's fees, and expenses incurred by the persons who attended the conference.

Not all mediation sessions are alike. Some mediators are very active in their efforts to come up with solutions and persuade the parties to resolve custody disputes while others will sit back and do little more than referee the parties' conversations.

Mediation conferences are private and confidential, except for threats of harm or attempts to inflict physical harm made during the conference, any disclosures required by law to be reported, or any information the parties agree to disclose.

Status Conferences

Family Court judges sometimes schedule status conferences when a case has been on the docket for a while but is not yet scheduled for a final hearing. If a status conference is called, the lawyers for both sides will have a brief meeting with a Family Court judge to discuss what needs to be done before the case is ready for a hearing. Often, a hearing date is set during a status conference. The judge does not make any rulings about the case during a status conference, and no official record of the meeting is made.

Trial

After all pleadings are filed and any discovery is completed, a final hearing can be requested. The lawyers will coordinate their schedules. One of them will notify the Family Court Clerk that the case is ready for a final hearing, tell the Clerk how much time the lawyers think it will take to try the case, and inform the Clerk of any scheduling conflicts that exist. The Clerk will then put the case on the trial schedule. In most counties, if the parties request more than two hours of court time, the Chief Administrative judge for the circuit will schedule a pretrial conference to try to narrow the issues and shorten the time needed for the trial.

Once the Clerk has set the case for trial, it is the plaintiff's responsibility to serve notice of the hearing on the defendant and to file proof that service was accomplished. In some counties, the Clerk will send out notices to both sides. When the trial date is set is also when trial subpoenas are often issued to witnesses.

In cases in which adultery, physical cruelty, or habitual drunkenness is the basis for requesting a divorce, a final hearing cannot be scheduled within less than 60 days after the complaint is filed, and the trial judge cannot issue an order of divorce in less than 90 days. If the ground for divorce is separation for one year or desertion, a final hearing can be scheduled as soon as the Clerk can find a time on the trial docket once an answer has been filed or the time for filing one has run.

Final Hearing

The final hearing is when both sides have an opportunity to present evidence about any disputes the Family Court is asked to resolve or about any other relevant topic. If there are not any disputed issues, the judge will simply decide whether sufficient evidence exists to establish a ground for divorce and whether to approve any agreements of the parties.

➤ What Will Happen During the Hearing

Family Court judges are required by law to try to reconcile the parties, if possible, so all final divorce hearings begin with the judge asking each party if there is anything the judge can to do help them save the marriage. Although the responses of both parties are usually negative, people occasionally drop their divorce actions and reconcile at the final hearing. You should think about this before the hearing and tell your lawyer if you think reconciliation is possible.

If there are no contested issues and the divorce is based on one-year separation (this is what happens in most cases), the hearing will begin with the plaintiff going to the witness stand and taking an oath to tell the truth. The plaintiff will then briefly tell the Court when the marriage occurred, when the separation happened, that the parties have lived separate and apart for more than one year without cohabitation, and that he or she wants a divorce and any other relief requested in the pleadings (for example, the wife might want to resume using her maiden name).

If the parties have reached an agreement that they want the Family Court to approve, the judge or the plaintiff's lawyer will ask questions to establish that the plaintiff understands the terms of the agreement and freely and voluntarily entered into it. The defendant's lawyer seldom asks any questions of the plaintiff.

Following the plaintiff will be a witness for the plaintiff whose only purpose is to corroborate the fact that the plaintiff and the defendant lived separate and apart for more than a year without cohabitation. This will conclude the plaintiff's case.

The defendant is not required to be present unless the parties have reached an agreement that they want the judge to approve. If the parties are asking the judge to approve an agreement, the defendant will briefly take the stand to testify in response to questions from the judge or the defendant's lawyer to establish that the defendant understands the terms of the agreement and freely and voluntarily entered into it.

If the ground for divorce is something other than a one-year separation, the plaintiff's lawyer will call witnesses and introduce any other evidence that tends to establish that the defendant committed whatever kind of marital misconduct is serving as the ground for divorce. If the defendant is not contesting the ground for divorce, the defendant may also take the stand to admit engaging in marital misconduct. If the judge is not persuaded that the plaintiff proved that a ground for divorce exists, the judge will treat the divorce action as though it was an action for separate support and maintenance and can decide any contested issues between the parties, such as property division, child custody, or support. The party who wants the divorce will then have to wait until a one-year period of separation has run before filing for divorce again.

If there are contested matters between the parties, the lawyers will call witnesses and introduce other evidence to try to persuade the Family Court to grant the relief that their clients want. Family Court hearings are similar to trials in all other courts, although some of the rules are relaxed somewhat and there is never a jury. The judge decides what the facts are and determines what legal conclusions to draw from them. Using the testimony of children is heavily discouraged but sometimes cannot be avoided.

At the conclusion of the hearing, the judge will either announce the judge's rulings or take the case under advisement. If a case is taken under advisement, the judge will inform both lawyers as soon as a decision is made.

➤ How to Behave During the Trial

Your lawyer will probably tell you how to prepare for and how to behave during the trial. If so, you should follow the lawyer's instructions, even if the purpose is not entirely clear. Some of the more common instructions to clients are set out below.

You should dress nicely for any court appearances. Judges will evaluate you in part by the way you dress, and certainly by the way you act in court. Sunday church clothes are not required, but they would be appropriate. Don't wear too much makeup or jewelry. Don't chew gum. Stand and sit erectly; don't slouch.

Pay attention to what the judge says. Look at the judge when you speak, and speak clearly and slowly enough for the judge and the court reporter to understand what you are saying. Refer to the judge as "your honor." Don't lose your temper, especially not at the judge, no matter what happens.

If there are contested issues in the case, it is especially important to listen carefully to each question presented to you, then pause before answering to be sure you understand the question and know what to say. If either lawyer says "I object," you should stop talking until the judge rules on the objection and instructs you whether to answer the question.

If you do not know the answer to a question, say "I don't know." Never lie. Tell the absolute truth, even if you fear it will hurt your case, but do not volunteer information. When you have answered the question, stop talking.

Be as polite as you possibly can be. Say "yes sir" or "yes ma'am" and "no sir" or "no ma'am." Do not be rude or snippy, even when responding to your spouse's lawyer, whose objective may be to get you to appear rude or snippy.

Final Order

Once a judge announces a final decision, the judge will usually ask that a proposed order be drafted by the lawyer for the plaintiff in an uncontested case or by the lawyer whose client prevails in a contested case. The lawyer who drafts the order will give the other lawyer a chance to review it and suggest revisions. It will then be sent to the judge for the judge's approval and signature. No action by the Family Court is final until an order has been signed by the judge and filed with the Clerk of Court. The final order is supposed to be prepared within 30 days of the final hearing.

The Family Court Clerk will file the order once it is signed by the judge and provide a copy for the lawyer of the prevailing side. If a divorce or annulment was granted by the judge, the Clerk will also file a form with the Bureau of Vital Statistics that creates an official, public record of the divorce. The lawyer for the plaintiff is expected to prepare the vital statistics form for the Clerk.

The lawyer for the prevailing side is expected to make sure that the opposing party receives a copy of the final order.

After the Final Order is Filed

Post-Trial Motions

After a final order is received from the trial judge, both parties have ten days to ask the judge to reconsider or revise the order. The parties cannot raise new issues in post-trial motions, but they may ask the judge to rule on issues that were raised but not ruled on in the order (a failure to make such a request means that any issues that were not ruled on by the trial judge cannot be ruled on by an appellate court if the case is appealed). A post-trial motion may also ask the Family Court to amend its findings or to make additional findings and to amend the order accordingly.

Another type of post-trial motion allows courts to correct mistakes arising from oversight or omission up to one year after the order is received. This includes mistakes, inadvertence, surprise, excusable neglect, newly discovered evidence that could not be discovered at the time of trial, fraud or other misconduct, and so forth.

In many cases, a motion to reconsider must be made to the trial court before an appeal is allowed.

Appeals

A notice of intention to appeal must be filed within 30 days after receiving the Family Court's final order, which may be the divorce decree or the order of the Family Court disposing of any post-trial motions. After the trial ends, you should discuss the advisability of appealing any adverse rulings with your attorney at the earliest possible moment. If a lawyer represented you at trial, the lawyer should be willing to file a notice of appeal for you, if you insist, even if the lawyer does not believe you will prevail on appeal.

Appeals are a specialty area of law practice, and you should not try to handle your own appeal. A lawyer's assistance is virtually imperative. Some divorce lawyers do not handle appeals. They refer their clients to other lawyers who specialize in appellate practice. If your divorce lawyer does not want to handle the appeal, ask the lawyer to give you the names of several lawyers who specialize in appeals and do not delay in getting one of those lawyers to evaluate your prospects.

Before you hire any lawyer to represent you on appeal, including your divorce lawyer, you should ask how many appeals the lawyer has taken and how many of them were successful. Appeals from trial decisions are fairly rare in divorce litigation, but an experienced lawyer should have some record in the appellate courts. You should try to avoid hiring a lawyer who has never handled an appeal. Do not be afraid to do some comparison shopping for an appellate lawyer, just as you did in searching for the right divorce lawyer.

Appeals from Family Court decisions will usually be heard by the Court of Appeals of South Carolina, although the Supreme Court of South Carolina sometimes takes jurisdiction over cases that present particularly important issues of law. Whichever court hears the appeal can make its own conclusions of law and findings of facts based on the record of the case (pleadings, evidence, and transcript). No new evidence can be submitted to the appellate court, nor may issues be raised on appeal that were not presented to the Family Court judge. It is common for appeals to take over a year before the appellate court announces its decision.

While an order of the Family Court is being appealed, some of the portions of the Family Court's order that are being challenged will go into effect and become enforceable right away while other parts of the order may be stayed, that is, they will not become effective and enforceable until the appeal is finished.

Child custody and visitation orders are not stayed by an appeal. Therefore, if the Family Court awards custody to the father and the mother appeals this ruling, the children will live with the father while the appeal is pending. It does not matter where the children were living when the Family Court issued its order.

Spousal and child support orders are not stayed by appeals, and they must be paid during the appeal. This would include payment of college expenses, if any were ordered. If the appellate court decides that too much support was ordered, it may require the excess amount to be repaid, perhaps with interest.

If a money judgment (such as a specific amount of cash awarded in a property division or a spousal or child support award) is not paid while an appeal is pending, interest will accrue at an interest rate that is currently set by law at 12% per year.

Property division orders are stayed by appeals. If a Family Court judge orders the parties to sell property, and one of the parties appeals, the sale or transfer cannot take place while the appeal is pending unless it is lifted by order of the trial judge or the appellate court.

When an appellate court decides an appeal from the Family Court, it will usually either affirm or reverse the Family Court's rulings. The appellate courts are aware that it takes a long time for cases to work their way through the judicial system, and they prefer to make decisions in Family Court cases that will bring finality to disputes between divorcing spouses and enable people to get on with their lives as soon as possible. Sometimes this is not possible, for example, when the appellate court does not believe the information presented at trial was sufficient for it to make a fair ruling. In such cases, it may remand the case and instruct the Family Court to conduct additional hearings and make additional rulings. After the Family Court does this, a person who is unhappy with the result may decide to file another appeal and start the process all over again.

CHAPTER FOUR

Issues That Frequently Arise
When a Marriage Ends

Family Violence

Introduction: You Are Not Alone

Violent behavior is too frequently a factor in the dissolution of marriages, either as a cause for the breakdown of marital relations or as a byproduct of the divorce process. Marriage and divorce can be very intense emotional experiences and some people react violently. As a result, some dissolving families experience physical abuse of spouses and children, rape, stalking, harassment, and other forms of violent behavior.

Family violence is a serious criminal justice and public health concern. It affects victims, perpetrators, and bystanders, who most commonly are children or other family members. The effects on survivors and their families include physical injury and disability, temporary chronic psychological harm, damage to social networks, and devastating economic loss, such as unemployment, property damage, and loss of housing. Children exposed to domestic violence wear psychological scars that are often manifested as behavioral problems or learning disabilities.

If you or a member of your family is the victim of violence at the hands of another family member, you are not alone. Family violence is pervasive in U.S. society. In South Carolina, 1 in 4 women and 1 in 8 men will suffer from intimate partner violence at some time during their lives. South Carolina has one of the highest rates of domestic violence in the country, including the rate of women killed by men. Domestic violence occurs among husbands and wives, former spouses, parents, siblings, children, grandparents, grandchildren, in-laws, stepparents, stepchildren, stepsiblings, other family members, boyfriends and girlfriends, children of boyfriends and girlfriends, children cared for by babysitters, and homosexual partners.

Although women or men may be assaulted in a domestic dispute, women account for 84% of those treated for injuries by intimate partners. The most commonly reported weapons in domestic violence are personal weapons, such as hands, feet, fists, elbows, etc. The most commonly reported location of domestic violence is the residence or home.

Fortunately, there are laws and support systems in place to help protect family members from violence. Unfortunately, there is no guarantee that these measures will be effective in any given situation. However, your risks of becoming a victim of violence can be reduced by reporting incidents to law enforcement officials and taking other legal action, using victim support services, and making adjustments in your daily activities.

Physical Violence

Physical violence against a spouse can serve as a ground for divorce (see the section in Chapter Two on divorce grounds). Physical violence against a spouse or a child can also serve as the basis of a lawsuit to recover damages for injuries and pain and suffering, and violence against family members is a crime that can lead to imprisonment. Thus, the same violent activity can serve as a basis for putting someone in jail (the state is the offended party when a law is broken), for ordering a person to pay money to someone they hurt (the injured person is the offended party when personal violence occurs), and for allowing a person subjected to violence by a spouse to get out of the marriage (the courts will not force a person to continue living with someone who is violent).

➤ Definitions of Violent Behavior and Criminal Penalties

The most effective deterrent to violence directed at family members is enforcement of the criminal laws, primarily the laws prohibiting criminal domestic abuse and sexual abuse, although a person engaging in violent acts may also be guilty of assault, assault and battery, assault and battery of a high and aggravated nature, or other criminal offenses.

There are four levels of criminal domestic violence defined by South Carolina law. These are, in descending order of severity, criminal domestic violence of a high and aggravated nature, and criminal domestic violence in the first, second, or third degree. There are also separate crimes of criminal sexual conduct in the first and second degrees and spousal sexual battery as well as criminal sexual conduct with minor children and incest, which are forms of domestic violence when committed against a family member. Each of these crimes is discussed below.

The "family members" who are protected by the domestic violence laws include spouses, former spouses, persons who have a child in common, and a male and female who are cohabiting or formerly have cohabited.

Short of murder, the most serious form of domestic violence is **criminal domestic violence of a high and aggravated nature**. Criminal domestic violence of a high and aggravated nature is a felony. A person is guilty of criminal violence of a high and aggravated nature when the person:

- commits the offense under circumstances manifesting extreme indifference to the value of human life and great bodily injury occurs,

- commits the offense, with or without an accompanying battery and under circumstances manifesting extreme indifference to the value of human life, and would reasonably cause a person to fear imminent great bodily injury or death, or

- violates a protection order and, in the process of violating the order, commits domestic violence in the first degree.

Circumstances that manifest an extreme indifference to human life include, but are not limited to the following:

- using a deadly weapon,

- knowingly and intentionally impeding the normal breathing or circulation of the blood of a household member by applying pressure to the throat or neck or by obstructing the nose or mouth of a household member and thereby causing stupor or loss of consciousness for any period of time,

- committing the offense in the presence of a minor,

- committing the offense against a person he knew, or should have known, was pregnant,

- committing the offense during the commission of a robbery, burglary, kidnapping, or theft, or

- using physical force against another to block that person's access to any cell phone, telephone, or electronic communications device with the purpose of preventing, obstructing, or interfering with the report of a crime to a law enforcement agency or a request for an ambulance or emergency medical assistance.

A person who is convicted of domestic abuse of a high and aggravated nature can be imprisoned for up to 20 years. Also, it is unlawful for a person convicted of this crime to ship, transport, receive, or possess a firearm or ammunition.

Criminal domestic violence is defined as causing physical harm or injury to a person's own household member or offering or attempting to cause harm to a household member, with apparent present ability, under circumstances reasonably creating fear of imminent peril. That is, a person can be arrested just for threatening harm to a family member or acting in a way that causes a reasonable person to believe they are about to be harmed.

There are three levels of criminal domestic violence.

Criminal domestic violence of the first degree is a felony that can be punished with imprisonment for up to ten years. It is unlawful for a person convicted of domestic violence of the first degree to ship, transport, receive, or possess a firearm or ammunition.

Criminal domestic violence of the second degree is a misdemeanor. The penalty for committing this crime is a fine of not less than two thousand five hundred dollars ($2,500) nor more than five thousand dollars ($5,000) or imprisonment for up to three years, or both. It is unlawful for a person convicted of domestic violence of the second degree to ship, transport, receive, or possess a firearm or ammunition, if the Court made specific findings that the person caused moderate bodily injury to a household member or if the judge ordered that the person be prohibited from doing these things.

Criminal domestic violence in the third degree is a misdemeanor, and a person who commits this crime must be fined not less than one thousand dollars ($1,000) nor more than two thousand five hundred dollars ($2,500) or imprisoned not more than 90 days, or both. It is unlawful for a person convicted of domestic violence of the third degree to ship, transport, receive, or possess a firearm or ammunition if the judge ordered that the person be prohibited from doing these things.

Criminal sexual conduct involves engaging in the following acts without the other person's consent: sexual intercourse, cunnilingus, fellatio, anal intercourse, or any intrusion, however slight, of any part of a person's body or of any object into the genital or anal openings of another person's body. Such acts constitute sexual battery.

Criminal sexual conduct in the first degree is a felony punishable by imprisonment for up to 30 years. A person is guilty of criminal sexual battery in the first degree if the person engages in sexual battery and any of the following circumstances are proven:

1. the perpetrator uses physical force of a high and aggravated nature;

2. the victim suffers sexual battery where the victim is also being subjected to forcible confinement, kidnapping, trafficking in persons, robbery, extortion, burglary, housebreaking, or any other similar offense;

3. the perpetrator causes the victim to become mentally or physically incapacitated by causing the victim to take a controlled or any intoxicating substance.

Criminal sexual conduct in the second degree is a felony punishable by up to 20 years in prison. A person is guilty of criminal sexual battery in the second degree if the person uses aggravated coercion to accomplish sexual battery.

Criminal sexual conduct in the third degree is a felony punishable by up to ten years in prison. A person is guilty of criminal sexual battery in the third degree if the person uses force or coercion to accomplish a sexual battery in the absence of aggravating circumstances or the actor knows or has reason to know that the victim is mentally defective or incapacitated, or physically helpless, and aggravated force or coercion was not used to accomplish the battery.

Assault with **intent** to commit criminal sexual conduct can be punished the same as if the crime of criminal sexual conduct was committed.

A person cannot be convicted of criminal sexual assault if the victim is the legal spouse unless the couple is living apart and the offending spouse's conduct constitutes criminal sexual conduct in the first or second degree. In order to prosecute a legal spouse for criminal sexual conduct, the crime must be reported to law enforcement officials within 30 days.

A spouse can be charged with **spousal sexual battery** only when a couple is living together. It is committed when one spouse uses aggravated force (that is, uses or threatens to use a weapon or uses or threatens to use physical force or physical violence of a high and aggravated nature) to make the other spouse engage in sexual intercourse, cunnilingus, fellatio, anal intercourse, or any intrusion, however slight, of any part of a person's body or of any object into the genital or anal openings of another person's body. In order to prosecute a person for spousal sexual battery the crime must be reported to law enforcement officials within 30 days. Upon conviction, a person may be imprisoned for up to ten years.

Criminal sexual conduct with minor children is a separate crime, and the severity of the penalty depends on the age of the child. It is not a crime to engage in consensual sexual relations with a child over the age of 16 unless it involves incest.

Incest (sexual relations with a person closely related by blood or marriage as defined by state law) is a separate crime for which a person can be sentenced to up to ten years in prison. Thus, sexual relations between a parent and a child or stepchild (or other people closely related by blood or marriage) is a crime irrespective of the person's age.

How to Respond to the Risk of Violence

➤ **Establish a Safety Plan**

The most important thing is to do whatever you can to protect yourself, your children, and other family members from violence. You should develop a plan for avoiding the risk of violence.

Help can be obtained by calling the National Domestic Violence Hotline at 800-799-SAFE (800-799-7233), and the National Center for Victims of Crime 202-467-8700.

There is a list of resources related to domestic violence that can be found online at www.lawhelp.org/sc/issues/domestic-violence.

Many of the suggestions for avoiding domestic violence are the same as those for responding to stalking or harassment, which are discussed later in this chapter.

If you or family members are threatened with violence or attacked, you should immediately call 911 for police assistance. If you are attacked inside a building, try to get outside, if possible, or at least try to stay away from the kitchen or other areas where weapons such as knives are present. After the attack ends, call the police, seek medical help, and take pictures of any injuries or property damage.

You should also consult with a lawyer to learn about other potential legal remedies.

➤ Get Help

● Hotlines, Websites, and Shelters

In addition to police help, there are a variety of victim support services available to people who are at risk of family violence. The South Carolina Department of Social Services (DSS) administers a program designed to prevent or reduce the incidence of domestic violence and to provide assistance for victims of violence. DSS provides funding for domestic violence intervention agencies. DSS provides a wide variety of services to victims of domestic violence.

A system of regional emergency shelters has been established. These shelters provide: 24 hour crisis lines, client needs assessments, information and referral services, temporary emergency shelters, daycare for children, individual and group counseling, legal advocacy, and assistance with obtaining housing and employment.

People are eligible for services from the shelters without regard to income, gender, or national origin. Fees may be charged for services with prior approval of the Department of Social Services but services cannot be denied for nonpayment. Service providers and contact information are available on the DSS website at https://dss.sc.gov. Or you can call DSS' domestic violence program at 803-898-7318.

Local telephone numbers are located in most phone books under "domestic abuse" and other headings. There are also some toll-free national abuse hotlines. The number for the National Domestic Violence Hotline is 800-799-SAFE (800-799-7233), and the National Center for Victims of Crime can be reached at 202-467-8700. Both of these organizations can help locate local shelters and obtain other assistance.

The following three websites provide useful information:

1. The National Coalition Against Domestic Violence website at www.ncadv.org has information about safety planning, victim support, and workplace guidelines.

2. The American Bar Association Commission on Domestic Violence website at www.americanbar.org/groups/ domestic_violence.html also has information about safety planning and other resources.

3. The South Carolina Coalition Against Domestic Violence and Sexual Assault website at www.sccadvasa.org has similar information and links to numerous other sites.

- **Orders of Protection and Other Relief From the Family Court**

An order of protection is a court order that directs the person to stay away from you and leave you alone. An order of protection does not provide a guarantee that the person being restrained will stop engaging in violence. It is simply a piece of paper, and you should remain alert and continue following your safety plan after an order of protection is issued. On the other hand, many people do comply with orders of protection. If they do not they are at risk of immediate arrest. Additionally, violators can be held in contempt of court and be sentenced to a term in jail or fined, or both.

Once an order of protection has been issued and served, law enforcement officers are allowed to arrest anyone who violates the order. No warrant is required. If you obtain an order of protection, keep it with you at all times. This will enable law enforcement officers to act more decisively if you need help. Also give a copy to your employer and neighbors so they can summon help, if needed. If the order includes protection for your children, give a copy to your children's daycare providers and schools.

A victim of domestic abuse can obtain an order of protection from the Family Court under the Protection From Domestic Abuse Act. A petition for an order of protection can be made by any household member in need of protection or by any household member on behalf of minor household members (a person cannot petition for a protective order for a child if the child is 18 years old or older). The assistance of an attorney is not required, although it may be helpful. If your spouse has any assets, the Family Court may be willing to order your spouse to pay your attorneys' fees and costs.

The Clerk of the Family Court in each county will provide simple forms to make it easier for victims who are not represented by counsel to file petitions. No filing fee is charged for filing a petition for an order of protection from domestic abuse.

There are instructions regarding how to seek an order of protection from the Family Court online at www.sccourts.org and www.lawhelp.org/sc/issues/domestic-violence.

The petition should allege abuse of a household member, stating specific times, places, and details of the abuse. If a divorce action or an action for separate support and maintenance is pending, the petition for protection from domestic abuse should be brought as a motion in that proceeding and served on the opposing counsel of record, if there is one, or on the opposing party.

An emergency hearing may be held within 24 hours for good cause shown (good cause includes a statement of facts showing an immediate and present danger of bodily harm verified by supporting affidavits). If the Court denies a 24-hour hearing or if one was not requested, the petitioner (the person filing the action) may request a hearing within 15 days of the filing of the petition. A copy of the petition will be served by the Court on the respondent (the person accused of domestic abuse) at least five days before the hearing if it is not an emergency hearing. If the respondent is not served, he or she is entitled to a continuance.

An order of protection will be issued if the Court finds that domestic violence has occurred. An order for protection may:

1. temporarily order the respondent not to abuse, threaten to abuse, or molest the petitioner or persons on whose behalf the petition was filed.

2. temporarily order the respondent not to communicate with or attempt to communicate with the petitioner or persons on whose behalf the petition was filed.

3. temporarily order the respondent not to enter or attempt to enter the petitioner's place of residence, employment, education, or other location the court orders.

The Family Court judge may also include in an order of protection:

1. an award of temporary custody or visitation rights over children who are in the parties' custody.

2. a provision directing the respondent to pay temporary support for the petitioner and children.

3. permission for the petitioner to have temporary exclusive possession of the parties' residence.

4. a prohibition for either party to dispose of or encumber any real or personal property mutually owned by the parties or in which a party claims an equitable interest.

5. permission for one party to have temporary possession of personal property.

6. a requirement that one party pay the other party's attorneys' fees and costs.

7. other relief as authorized by law, including an order requiring the sheriff's department or police department to accompany the petitioner and assist the petitioner in gaining possession of the dwelling or to assist otherwise in the execution of the order.

An Order of Protection From Domestic Abuse stays in effect for a fixed time of not less than six months nor more than a year. The time may be extended or terminated by the Court. If the parties reconcile, the petitioner may dismiss the order without a hearing by signing a written request to dismiss based on the reconciliation.

Stalking and Harassment

Stalking and harassment are crimes. The difference between stalking and harassment is one of degree. The crimes may encompass similar acts, but their effect upon the target is the key difference. When the victim feels mental distress, and a reasonable person would feel similarly under the circumstances as a result of the activities, he or she is being harassed. If the victim fears bodily harm to herself or members of her family, and a reasonable person would feel this way, the victim is being stalked.

A Department of Justice study showed that women are the victims in 90% of stalking cases. Although stalking cases involving celebrities are widely known, more than 80% of victims are ordinary people. There are two main categories of stalkers according to psychologists. Love obsession stalkers are fixated on a person with whom they have no personal relationship. Simple obsession stalkers (the majority at about 75%) have had a previous relationship with their targets. One out of twenty adults will be stalked in their lifetimes.

Stalking is a serious crime that too frequently escalates into violence. One in 12 women and one in 45 men will be stalked in their lifetimes. Do not assume that a stalker will quickly lose interest and go away. The average duration of stalking is 1.8 to 2.2 years.

➤ Definitions of Harassment and Criminal Penalties

Criminal harassment means a pattern of intentional, substantial, and unreasonable intrusion into the private life of a targeted person that serves no legitimate purpose and causes the person and would cause a reasonable person in his position to suffer mental or emotional distress. It must involve two or more acts occurring over a period of time, however short, evidencing a continuity of purpose.

Harassment in the first degree may include, but is not limited to:

1. following the targeted person from location to location;

2. visual or physical contact that is initiated, maintained, or repeated after a person has been given oral or written notice that the contact is unwanted or after the victim has filed an incident report with a law enforcement agency;

3. surveillance of or the maintenance of a presence near the targeted person's residence, place of work, school, or any other place regularly occupied or visited by the targeted person; and

4. vandalism and property damage.

Harassment in the first degree is a misdemeanor and the penalty is a fine of up to one thousand dollars ($1,000), a sentence of up to three years, or both. The fine can be up to two thousand dollars ($2,000) if the harassment violated a restraining order. If the perpetrator had a prior conviction for harassment or stalking within ten years, harassment in the first degree is a felony, and the penalty is a fine of up to five thousand dollars ($5,000), a sentence of up to five years, or both.

Harassment in the second degree may include, but is not limited to, verbal, written, or electronic contact that is initiated, maintained, or repeated.

Harassment in the second degree is a misdemeanor, and the penalty is a fine of up to two hundred dollars ($200), a sentence of up to 30 days, or both. The penalty can be up to one thousand dollars ($1,000) and the sentence can be up to one year, or both, if the harassment violated a restraining order or if the perpetrator had a prior conviction for harassment or stalking within ten years.

➤ Definitions of Stalking and Criminal Penalties

The **crime of stalking** means a pattern of intentional, substantial, and unreasonable intrusion into the private life of a targeted person that serves no legitimate purpose and causes the person and would cause a reasonable person in the targeted person's position to fear:

1. death of the person or a member of his family,

2. assault upon the person or a member of his family,

3. bodily injury to the person or a member of his family,

4. criminal sexual conduct on the person or a member of his family,

5. kidnapping of the person or a member of his family, or

6. damage to the property of the person or a member of his family.

Like criminal harassment, stalking must involve two or more acts occurring over a period of time, however short, evidencing a continuity of purpose. "Family" means a spouse, child, parent, sibling, or a person who regularly resides in the same household as the targeted person.

Types of behaviors that might constitute stalking include the following:[5]

1. visiting or following the target and/or family,

2. making harassing phone calls,

3. sending threatening mail or email,

4. trespassing,

5. burglarizing,

6. vandalizing,

7. leaving items such as dead flowers,

8. killing or injuring pets,

9. unscrewing outside lights,

10. disabling alarms,

---

[5] This list is from Nicole Howland, *What You Need to Know About Stalking*, HOT TIPS FROM THE BEST DOMESTIC LAW PRACTITIONERS (S.C. Bar - CLE Division 1999).

11. disabling cars,

12. disabling telephones,

13. planting listening devices,

14. filing a change of address form at Post Office to intercept mail, or

15. disconnecting electric or gas service.

Stalking is a felony, and the penalty is a fine of up to five thousand dollars ($5,000), imprisonment for up to five years, or both. If the stalking is in violation of a restraining order, the penalty increases to up to seven thousand dollars ($7,000), imprisonment for up to ten years, or both. A person who engages in stalking within ten years of a prior conviction of harassment or stalking is guilty of a felony, and the penalty could be a fine of up to ten thousand dollars ($10,000), imprisonment for up to 15 years, or both.

How to Respond to Stalking and Harassment

➤ Establish a Safety Plan

You should take steps to learn more about how to discourage the perpetrator and to protect yourself and your family from harm. The National Center for Victims of Crime has a stalking resource center. Online at www.victimsofcrime.org/our-programs/stalking-resource-center. Telephone: 202-467-8700. Email: src@ncvc.org.

The most commonly given first piece of advice is to cut off all forms of communication with the harasser/stalker. Do not talk to him or her on the telephone or in person, or even respond to email messages. Consider changing your telephone number to an unlisted number or purchasing caller identification or call block service. You may also want to get a private mail box that is not at the post office and file a change of address listing the box. Destroy discarded mail (buy a shredder). If you think the stalker has your Social Security number and is using it to find you or for other improper purposes, consider checking with the Social Security Administration to see if you can change your Social Security number.

It is also important to document what is happening. You may need to produce evidence of the misconduct at a court proceeding. Record incidents in a diary, record any threatening calls, or even make a video of the misbehavior. If you do not change your telephone number, ask the telephone company if it can help you track where telephone calls are coming from and to document how often they occur. Use an answering machine to record harassing calls or have a friend listen to the calls. Make a log.

The most important thing is to protect yourself and other family members. Secure your home. Consider installing a burglar alarm. Keep lights on indoors and outdoors. Get a dog. Trim shrubbery around your house. Tell trusted neighbors what is happening and ask them to be alert (give them a picture or description of the stalker and his or her vehicle). Require service people to show identification before allowing them to enter your house. Try not to be home alone. Buy a cell phone so you will be able to call for help if your telephone lines are cut. Accompany your children to and from school or the bus stop.

At work, alert security personnel and trusted coworkers about the situation and give them pictures or descriptions of the person. Park in a secured area or ask security personnel to escort you to and from your office.

You should be especially alert when you are in your car. Always keep the windows up and the doors locked and do not let the gas level get too low. Consider installing locks on gas caps and hoods. Only park in well-lit and secure areas. Do not get in your car without first looking inside. Vary the routes you take to work and when running errands. If you think you are being followed, drive to the nearest police station (know where the stations are located). Whenever you go out, try not to go out alone and stay in public areas.

➤ Get Help

• Law Enforcement

The first thing to do is to call 911 and report the crime to law enforcement. According to South Carolina law, the primary responsibility of a law enforcement officer when responding to a harassment or stalking incident is to enforce the law and protect the complainant. A person who reports harassment or stalking, files a criminal complaint, seeks a restraining order, or participates in judicial proceeding in good faith is immune from civil or criminal liability.

You should also consult with a lawyer to learn about other potential legal remedies.

• Restraining Orders From Magistrate's Court

A restraining order is a court order that directs the person to stay away from you and leave you alone. A restraining order does not provide a guarantee that the person being restrained will stop engaging in stalking or harassment. It is simply a piece of paper, and you should remain alert and continue following your safety plan after a restraining order is issued. On the other hand, many people do comply with restraining orders. If they do not they are at risk of immediate arrest. Additionally, violators can be held in contempt of court and be sentenced to a term in jail or fined, or both.

Once a restraining order has been issued and served, law enforcement officers are allowed to arrest anyone who violates the order. No warrant is required. If you obtain a restraining order, keep it with you at all times. This will enable law enforcement officers to act more decisively if you need help. Also give a copy to your employer and neighbors so they can summon help, if needed. If the order includes protection for your children, give a copy to your children's daycare providers and schools.

You may seek a restraining order in Magistrate's Court against a person who is engaging in harassment or stalking. A lawyer can help you obtain a restraining order, or you can do it yourself. Magistrate's Courts are required to provide forms to facilitate the preparation and filing of a complaint and motion if you do not have a lawyer (forms are also available at www.sccourts.org). The filing fee can be waived if you cannot afford to pay it.

After a petition for a restraining order is filed and served on the respondent, a hearing should be held within fifteen days but not sooner than five days after service. In extreme cases, an emergency hearing may be held within 24 hours after the petition is filed. A magistrate can issue a temporary restraining order without giving notice or holding a hearing, if you submit written affidavits with the petition showing that you are facing a present danger of bodily injury.

If emergency relief is granted, the temporary restraining order must be served upon the defendant within five days with a copy of the petition and a rule to show cause why it should not be extended for six months. The Magistrate's Court will provide for service of a restraining order on the respondent and will provide a copy to local law enforcement free of charge to the petitioner.

A restraining order issued by a magistrate dissolves in one year unless the Court has charged the defendant with the crime of harassment or stalking and has scheduled a date for the trial. If this has been done, the order remains in effect until the conclusion of the trial, at which time it may be extended.

Permanent Restraining Orders

Any victim of a crime (or a witness who aided in the prosecution of a crime) can seek a "Permanent Restraining Order" from the Circuit Court or the Family Court. This can be obtained by asking for the order at the time the offender is convicted of a criminal offense in Circuit Court or Family Court.

A permanent restraining order can also be obtained by filing a summons and complaint in the Court of Common Pleas. The Circuit Court is required to provide forms to facilitate the preparation and filing of the summons and complaint for a permanent restraining order by a complainant who is not represented by a lawyer. There is no fee charged for filing the complaint.

The hearing on the complaint can be conducted electronically by closed circuit television or other electronic means. A permanent restraining order remains in effect for a period of time to be determined by the judge.

Property Division

In General

Marital property is defined in South Carolina as all real estate and personal property that was acquired by the parties during the marriage and that is owned when marital litigation is commenced, regardless of how legal title is held.

When spouses cannot mutually agree how to divide their property, a Family Court has the power to do so in either a divorce action or a separate support and maintenance action, if either party requests this in the pleadings. When the Family Court divides property, it does so according to the rules of equitable apportionment that are established by statutory and case law. The philosophy of equitable apportionment is based on a recognition that marriage is, among other things, an economic partnership. Upon dissolution of the marriage, property accumulated during the marriage should be divided and distributed in a fair and equitable manner in consideration of factors set forth in state law.

The Family Court can only divide marital property as part of: (1) a divorce *a vinculo matrimonii*, (2) an action for separate support and maintenance, (3) a proceeding to dispose of marital property after a prior decree of dissolution of a marriage by a court that lacked personal jurisdiction over the other spouse or that lacked jurisdiction to dispose of the property, or (4) other marital litigation between the parties. The Family Court has jurisdiction to divide marital property only if division is requested in the pleadings by one of the parties.

The Family Court may not adjudicate property interests between people who are living together but not married. The Circuit Court of Common Pleas would be the appropriate forum.

Property owned by a third party can be equitably apportioned by the Family Court if the husband or wife claims an equitable interest in the property and the third party is made a party to the action.

The death of a spouse involved in marital litigation does not terminate proceedings to divide marital property.

The Family Court is expected to follow four steps in deciding how to divide marital property:

(1) identify the marital property, real and personal, to be divided between the parties;

(2) determine the fair market value of the property so identified;

(3) identify the proportionate contributions, both direct and indirect, of each party to the acquisition of the marital property; and

(4)   provide for an equitable division of the marital property.

Each of these four steps is discussed below.

Identification (What Is It?)

Marital property is all property accumulated during the marriage that does not fall within some established exception. Gifts of property from one spouse to the other during the marriage are marital property subject to division. Marital property includes debts as well as assets.

A "marital estate" is established when a spouse files a divorce complaint or initiates other marital litigation. The marital estate that comes into existence with the commencement of marital litigation ceases to exist if the marital litigation is withdrawn or stricken before a final order is issued.

Property acquired during the marriage and owned when marital litigation is commenced is presumed to be marital property, and the party claiming otherwise has the burden of establishing the nonmarital character of the property.

The Family Court does not have authority to apportion nonmarital property. Once the Court determines that property is nonmarital, it has no jurisdiction to address its ownership or to deal with the property in any way. Nonmarital property includes property that was owned prior to the marriage and not converted into marital property during the marriage. Also, inherited property and gifts to one spouse by a third party are nonmarital property and are not subject to equitable apportionment.

A spouse can obtain an interest in nonmarital property that belongs to the other spouse in two ways. First, a spouse can acquire an interest in nonmarital property by doing something that increases the value of the property, for example, by helping remodel a house. Any increase in the value of nonmarital property during the marriage is nonmarital property, except to the extent the increase resulted from the efforts of the other spouse during the marriage. If the value of nonmarital property increases due to the efforts of the nonowning spouse, the spouse may acquire a "special equity" interest in the increased value of the property, and this increased value can be apportioned by the Family Court. An increase in the value of nonmarital property resulting from inflation or market fluctuation is not marital property and the nonowner spouse does not acquire a special equity interest in its increased value.

The second way for one spouse to acquire an interest in the other spouse's property is for the spouse who owns the nonmarital property to do something that shows an intention for the property to become marital property. When this happens, it is called "transmutation." Many types of evidence might persuade a Family Court judge that someone intended for property to become marital property, but the strongest evidence is some kind of public declaration that the property is "ours" rather than "mine." The appellate cases are inconsistent in their decisions concerning transmutation, so you should consult a lawyer if you have money or other nonmarital property that you want to keep in your name alone.

Evidence of transmutation can include placing the property in joint names, transferring the property to the other spouse as a gift, using the property exclusively for marital purposes, commingling the property with marital property, using marital funds to build equity in the property, or exchanging the property for marital property. This evidence is not necessarily conclusive of the owner's intent, however.

The Family Court will probably conclude that the owner of nonmarital property intended to transmute it into marital property where both spouses have assumed responsibility for debt attached to the property. The existence of joint indebtedness creates a presumption of an intent to transmute the property, and it is not necessary to show that both parties contributed toward discharging the debt (the relative contributions toward discharging debts may be taken into account by the trial judge in apportioning the property, however). If property is determined to be transmuted by the creation of a joint debt obligation, all of the property that secures the debt is transmuted.

Mere commingling of nonmarital property with marital property does not automatically transmute nonmarital property into marital property. For example, funds belonging to one spouse retain their character as nonmarital property as long as they are traceable, irrespective of whether they are kept in separate or in joint accounts. Similarly, the use of funds produced by a nonmarital asset, such as rental income from a house owned by one spouse prior to the marriage, does not transmute the income-producing property into marital property, nor would selling the rental house and buying another rental house with the proceeds. Simply using a house as the marital residence does not necessarily transmute it into nonmarital property.

Retirement benefits, specifically civil service and military benefits, are marital assets subject to equitable division in South Carolina. Family Court judges are statutorily required to consider and weigh retirement benefits when apportioning marital property. Only the portion of retirement benefits that was earned during the marriage is subject to equitable apportionment.

Contributions to individual retirements accounts (IRA's) are subject to equitable distribution, if the contributions come from income earned during the marriage or from other marital property.

Social Security benefits cannot be reached for purposes of property division, either by agreement or court order. Courts have concluded that judges have no power to order one spouse to pay future Social Security benefits to the other spouse to effect property division, nor can they approve or enforce agreements between the parties to do so.

South Carolina state disability retirement benefits are income, not property subject to equitable distribution. The payments are not compensation for services performed during the marriage, rather, they are a replacement for income the disabled person would be earning currently and would be able to earn in the future had the disability not occurred.

Proceeds from employment claims that are received during the marriage before marital litigation is commenced are marital property subject to equitable division. Proceeds from personal injury claims are also subject to apportionment as marital property. Lottery winnings are also marital property.

Credit card charges incurred after the filing of marital litigation are not marital debts subject to equitable apportionment.

Valuation (What Is It Worth?)

The Family Court is required to determine the value of marital property. The Court's valuation of marital property cannot be arbitrary. A party may not complain on appeal that the trial court's valuation is unsupported by the evidence unless the party offered evidence about value at trial.

The date on which marital litigation is commenced is also the date on which the value of marital property is established. A valuation date other than the commencement of marital litigation may be used to avoid inequitable results, for example, when the parties are separated for a long time before commencing marital litigation or when a change in the value of the property during the litigation is attributable to one spouse's efforts alone.

When valuing a "going business" for purposes of equitable distribution in a divorce decree, the Court should value the assets as those of an on-going business and not as liquidated assets. Marital businesses are to be valued at fair market value as on-going businesses. The Court should accomplish its determination of the fair market value of the corporate property by considering the business' net asset value, the fair market value for its stock, and earnings or investment value.

In order to obtain equitable division of a retirement plan, the spouse claiming an interest must present evidence of the value of the retirement plan at the time of the marriage and at the time of the filing of the action. The value of retirement benefits are usually calculated by one of two methods: the present value method and the reserve jurisdiction method. The present value method is used when the Family Court can calculate what the value of the retirement fund was when marital litigation was filed. The Court then calculates the percentage of the present value attributable to the marriage and the appropriate equitable share of the other spouse. Usually, the pension is awarded to the employee spouse and there is an offset of other marital property to the nonemployee spouse. The present cash method promotes finality and the severance of the entanglements between the parties, but testimony from an expert witness, an actuary, is required to help the Family Court determine the present value.

The reserve jurisdiction method postpones the final division of the pension fund until a later date. The trial court determines the formula for division but delays actual distribution until benefit payments are actually being paid out.

Apportionment (How Much Should Each Spouse Get?)

Once the Family Court determines the identity of the marital property and what it is worth, it must then decide what percentage of it goes to each spouse. The Family Court is required to consider 15 factors in making this decision, but it is allowed to give weight to each factor in such proportion as it finds appropriate. The factors guide the Court in exercising its discretion over apportionment of the marital property. They are nothing more than equities to be considered in reaching a fair distribution of marital property. They subserve the ultimate goal of apportionment, which is to divide the marital estate, as a whole, in a manner that considers each spouse's contribution to the economic partnership and also the relative effect of ending that partnership on each of the parties.

The most important factor is often the **duration of the marriage**. If two people were married a long time, it is likely that their property will be divided 50-50. It is not clear exactly when a marriage will be considered long enough for the 50-50 presumption, but ten years is not considered to be a long marriage. The remaining 14 factors are:

1. **Marital misconduct or fault** of either or both parties (whether or not used as a basis for a divorce, if the misconduct affects or has affected the economic circumstances of the parties, or contributed to the breakup of the marriage),

2. The **contribution** of each spouse to the acquisition, preservation, depreciation, or appreciation in value of the marital property (including the contribution of a spouse as homemaker),

3. The **income** of each spouse, the earning potential of each spouse, and the opportunity for future acquisition of capital assets,

4. The **physical and emotional health** of each spouse,

5. The **need** of each spouse or either spouse **for additional training** or education in order to achieve that spouse's income potential,

6. The **nonmarital property** of each spouse,

7. The existence or nonexistence of **vested retirement benefits** for each or either spouse,

8. Whether **separate maintenance or alimony** has been awarded,

9. The desirability of **awarding the family home** as part of equitable distribution or the right to live therein for a reasonable period to the spouse having custody,

10. The **tax consequences** to each or either party as a result of any particular form of equitable apportionment,

11. The existence and extent of **any support obligations** of either party from a prior marriage or for any other reason or reasons,

12. **Liens and any other encumbrances** upon the marital property, which themselves must be equitably divided, or upon the separate property of either of the parties, and any other existing debts incurred by the parties or either of them during the marriage,

13. **Child custody arrangements** and obligations at the time of the order, and

14. Such **other relevant factors** as the trial court shall expressly enumerate in its order.

Property division may be affected by the manner in which the parties treat each other following their separation. If one party controls the assets and denies the other party fair access to them, the Family Court can take this into account in making an equitable division of marital property. When a spouse destroys or dissipates assets to prevent the other spouse from receiving a fair share of marital property, the full value of the marital property at the time marital litigation was commenced should be added to the marital estate, and the entire value of the wasted assets should be assessed against the wrongdoer's share of the marital estate, even if it will have severe consequences to the wrongdoer.

On the other hand, poor business decisions, in and of themselves, do not justify a downward modification of a party's entitlement to equitable distribution. Courts generally hold one spouse chargeable for depleting assets only where that spouse acts in bad faith with an intent to deprive the other spouse of marital assets.

Distribution (How to Divide It?)

The final step that a Family Court judge takes in dividing property is to decide which party gets which items of property. The judge may utilize any reasonable means to achieve equity between the parties. Absent compelling reasons, the objective in dividing marital property should be to sever all joint interests in the property as completely as possible. If possible, all issues between the parties should be resolved so that disputes and irritants do not linger and present further incentives to litigation. The Family Court's objective should be to sever all entangling legal relations and place the parties in a position from which they can begin anew. The parties should not be left in a position where they will be in business together.

The Family Court may employ any reasonable means to divide the property but the method used cannot be arbitrary. The Family Court has the power to require the sale of marital property and a division of the proceeds to effect an equitable apportionment, but it should first attempt an "in-kind" distribution of the assets before forcing a sale, that is, it should give each party various items of property with a total value equaling the amount that each party is awarded.

The Family Court has a broad array of tools at its disposal to aid it in identifying, protecting, and distributing the marital assets. It can take control of marital property, including ongoing businesses, at any stage of the proceedings where it appears to the Court that personal jurisdiction may not be obtained over an absent party or where a party refuses to comply with an order of the Court. The Family Court has the inherent power to appoint someone to take control of property to protect the interests of the parties. In addition to the option of sequestration, the Court is empowered to appoint a trustee, or even a receiver, when the parties are having trouble agreeing how to divide the property and it appears to the Court that one of the parties may be trying to waste or hide marital assets.

Tax Consequences

A transfer of property to a spouse incident to a divorce is not usually a taxable event. The person who transfers or receives the property will not be assessed with a gain or eligible to claim a loss. A transfer will be treated as incident to a divorce if it happens within one year of the end of the marriage or if it is related to the divorce and takes place not more than six years after the marriage ends. The same rule applies to transfers of property between spouses during the marriage.

Spousal Support (Alimony)

In General

Spousal support is money that one spouse is ordered to pay for the support of the other spouse when they are no longer living together. There is no difference between "alimony" and "separate support and maintenance," except that separate support and maintenance is what spousal support is called in actions for separate support and maintenance, and alimony is what it is called in divorce actions. The Family Court is required to allocate support between spousal support and child support.

It can be very difficult to predict whether spousal support will be awarded or how much. There is no set formula in South Carolina for determining whether a person is entitled to alimony nor for figuring out which type of alimony and how much of it should be awarded. The Family Court judges have a great deal of discretion. Some judges are more inclined to award spousal support than other judges. Even the most experienced lawyers must employ a great deal of guesswork in trying to predict alimony.

The justification for awarding spousal support has been explained as being founded on the natural and legal duty of one spouse to support the other spouse. This duty continues as long as they remain husband and wife. A person is not relieved of this duty by asking for or obtaining a divorce. Alimony has been called a substitute for the statutory right to marital support during marriage, and it has also been termed an allowance in lieu of a spouse's legal obligation to support the other spouse.

Although neither statutory law nor case law clearly explains why alimony is awarded, it is generally understood that the two primary justifications for alimony are to punish marital misconduct and to compensate the supported spouse for any of the following losses resulting from the marriage or divorce: loss in standard of living, loss of earnings arising from care of children, loss of earnings arising from care of third parties, loss due to investment in the other spouse's earning capacity, or unfair disparity in ability to recover pre-marital living standard after a brief marriage.

A party must ask for spousal support in the pleadings before the Family Court can award it. A spouse cannot come back to the Family Court in the future to ask for alimony for any reason after a divorce is granted, unless alimony was requested in the pleadings and the Court either awarded alimony or reserved the issue for future consideration. The only exception is when a spouse uses physical violence and threats to prevent the other spouse from seeking alimony.

The circumstances under which the Court can reserve spousal support for future consideration are narrow. The Family Court must determine that there exists an identifiable set of circumstances that is likely to generate a need for spousal support in the reasonably near future. Any reservation must be express and clear in the Court's order. If both parties agree that the question of alimony should be reserved, however, the Family Court can reserve alimony if it finds that reservation of alimony is within the bounds of reasonableness and is fair and equitable to both parties.

The Family Court can order someone to pay alimony even if that person does not live in South Carolina if the Court has obtained personal jurisdiction over the party. Personal jurisdiction is established either by consent of the party or by serving the party with legal process (e.g., a summons and complaint) in South Carolina. Personal jurisdiction can also be obtained by serving the party with pleadings outside of South Carolina or by publishing a notice in the newspaper (after obtaining permission from the Court), if the person has maintained sufficient minimum contacts with South Carolina that exercising such jurisdiction would not offend traditional notions of fair play and substantial justice. If you need to establish jurisdiction over someone who lives outside of South Carolina to seek alimony, you should consult with a lawyer.

Temporary Spousal Support

The Family Court is authorized to order one spouse to pay temporary spousal support while a divorce or separate support and maintenance action is pending. The principal objective of temporary spousal support is to give the spouse seeking support sufficient means for his or her support and to enable him or her to prosecute or defend the case. To this end, it is generally considered appropriate to award temporary alimony without making any investigation into the merits of the underlying cause if the spouse requesting support is unable to maintain himself or herself separately from the other spouse and the other spouse can afford to pay alimony. Thus, the principal inquiries at the temporary alimony hearing are related to the relative financial positions of the spouses rather than the cause of their separation.

If the Family Court later determines, however, that a spouse who was awarded temporary spousal support was not entitled to receive spousal support because of adultery or for some other reason, the supported spouse may be required to repay whatever payments were received.

Types of Spousal Support

> **In General**

There are six types of spousal support that may be awarded by the Family Court: (1) periodic alimony; (2) lump sum alimony; (3) rehabilitative alimony; (4) reimbursement alimony; (5) separate maintenance and support; and (6) such other form of spousal support, under terms and conditions as the Court may consider just, as appropriate under the circumstances without limitation to grant more than one form of support. Each type of alimony can be awarded temporarily or permanently.

Permanent periodic alimony is the form of alimony favored in South Carolina. The Family Court must determine that special circumstances exist before it can award any form of alimony other than periodic alimony, and the Family Court must make it clear which form of alimony is being awarded.

➤ Periodic Alimony

Permanent periodic alimony has been favored in South Carolina as a means of restoring a dependent spouse to the standard of living enjoyed during the marriage. Its purpose is to place the supported spouse, as nearly as practical, in the position of support he or she enjoyed during the marriage. It usually consists of monthly payments in cash.

Periodic alimony usually terminates on the remarriage of the supported spouse or upon the death of either spouse. Periodic alimony can be terminated or modified by the Family Court if circumstances change in the future. The changed circumstances must be significant and unanticipated.

➤ Lump Sum Alimony

Lump sum alimony is a finite total sum to be paid in one installment, or periodically over a period of time. It is awarded only in exceptional circumstances and for compelling reasons, such as where it appears that the paying spouse may not live up to regular alimony obligations. The principal justification given for awarding lump sum alimony is the unwillingness of the spouse ordered to provide support to make regular payments of periodic alimony and the existence of circumstances that would make it difficult to enforce a periodic alimony obligation, for example, when it seems likely that the obligor will move to another country. When it is awarded, lump sum alimony is nonmodifiable and terminates only upon the death of the supported spouse. It does not terminate upon remarriage of the supported spouse.

Although lump sum alimony is rarely awarded by the Family Court in contested cases, lump sum alimony is frequently approved when it is included in settlement agreements made by the parties.

➤ Rehabilitative Alimony

Rehabilitative alimony provides support for additional training or education to help a supported spouse achieve his or her income potential and to enable the supported spouse to become self-supporting. Rehabilitative alimony is not frequently awarded. Such awards are only valid in South Carolina when the evidence demonstrates a likelihood that the recipient will be self-sufficient at the expiration date of the ordered payments. Although the case law has not been consistent, most cases indicate that "self-sufficiency" means the ability to support oneself at the marital standard of living.

When rehabilitative alimony is awarded, it is terminable upon the remarriage of the supported spouse, the death of either spouse, or the occurrence of a specific event to occur in the future. It is modifiable based upon unforeseen events frustrating the good faith efforts of the supported spouse to become self-supporting or the ability of the supporting spouse to pay the rehabilitative alimony.

➤ Reimbursement Alimony

Reimbursement alimony essentially pays back one spouse who made extraordinary contributions that enhanced the earning potential of the other spouse, for example, by working to put the other spouse through college. It is to be paid in a finite sum, in one installment or periodically. It will terminate on the remarriage of the supported spouse, or upon the death of either spouse, but it is not terminable or modifiable based upon changed circumstances in the future.

➤ Separate Support and Maintenance

Separate support and maintenance is simply what spousal support is called when it is awarded in an action for separate support and maintenance rather than in a divorce action. This form of support may be awarded where a divorce is not sought but the Family Court believes it is necessary to provide support for a spouse when the parties are living separate and apart.

➤ Other Forms of Spousal Support

The Family Court is also permitted to award any other form of spousal support, irrespective of whether it is specifically mentioned elsewhere in the statute, under terms and conditions as the Court may consider just and appropriate under the circumstances. The Family Court may grant more than one form of spousal support.

Determining Entitlement and Amount

The Family Court judge has a great deal of discretion in deciding whether to award spousal support and how much. There is no set formula for determining whether a person is entitled to alimony nor for figuring out which type of alimony and how much of it should be awarded. The law requires the Family Court to consider a list of 13 factors before making its decision. The most significant factors in making decisions about spousal support can be grouped under three headings:

(1) the **duration of the marriage**. Longer marriages have a much higher probability of producing an alimony award than marriages of short duration. However, some spouses in relatively brief marriages have been awarded alimony.

(2) the **overall financial situation of the parties**, especially the ability or inability of the spouse requesting support to be self-supporting and the ability of the other spouse to pay alimony. If both parties are already equally capable of supporting themselves, there is no need for alimony. When a spouse is intentionally underemployed, the award of alimony will be based on that spouse's earning potential rather than his or her current reduced earnings.

(3) whether or not one of the parties was more at **fault** than the other in causing the breakdown of the marriage. Courts have come to recognize that when a marriage fails, both spouses are usually somewhat at fault in causing the deterioration of the marital relationship. However, a spouse will be denied support if he or she engages in substantial misconduct that materially contributes to the failure of the marriage, unless the other spouse is equally at fault. Consideration of fault is limited to misconduct that affects or has affected the economic circumstances of the parties or contributed to the breakup of the marriage.

In no event may fault be considered unless it occurred before (a) the formal signing of a written property or marital settlement agreement or (b) entry of a permanent order of separate maintenance and support or of a permanent order approving a property or marital settlement agreement between the parties. This even applies to adultery, which is otherwise an absolute bar to alimony. Also, adultery that has been condoned or unconditionally forgiven cannot be used as a basis for obtaining a divorce or for denying alimony.

Although the law is not entirely clear, the general rule is that in setting the amount of alimony the Family Court cannot consider the contributions of a spouse's relatives to his or her support. The reasoning behind this is that a supporting spouse has a legal duty to provide support whereas children and other relatives of a supported spouse have only a moral duty, thus the supporting spouse should not be relieved of a legal duty by the kindness of the supported spouse's relatives.

Method of Payment

In making an award of alimony or separate maintenance and support, the Family Court may order the supporting spouse to make the payments directly to the supported spouse, or it may require that the payments be made through the Family Court and add a service fee to the award. The Court may require the payment of debts, obligations, and other matters such as house payments and car payments on behalf of the supported spouse.

The normal rule is that spousal support is to be paid in cash and the Family Court should not order a supporting spouse to transfer property instead of money.

Tax Consequences

The general rule is that alimony and separate support and maintenance payments are taxed to the recipient and deducted by the payer, if the payments meet criteria set by the Internal Revenue Service (IRS). The most important criteria are that payments must be made in cash, the payer and payee may not be members of the same household at the time of payment, and the obligation must terminate upon the death or remarriage of the supported spouse. The IRS, however, allows the parties or the Family Court to designate the deductibility and taxability of alimony, that is, they have the power to deem alimony deductible to the payer spouse and taxable to the payee spouse. If a support award is not allocated between spousal and child support, the amount is taxable to the supported spouse and non-taxable to the supporting spouse. The advice of a professional is strongly recommended where any tax issues are involved.

Child Custody and Visitation

Who Is Entitled to Child Custody Absent a Court Order?

Although most child custody issues arise in the context of marital litigation, many custody disputes do not require judicial intervention. If parents can agree what custody arrangements are in the best interests of their children, the judicial system will usually stay out of the matter. Custody ceases to be an issue when a child reaches 18 years of age or otherwise becomes emancipated (see the section on duration of child support obligation later in this chapter).

Absent an agreement or court order regarding child custody, both parents are equally entitled to the custody of children born during the marriage. A statute provides that, absent a court order, the mother has the right to custody of children born out of wedlock, but this does not give the mother a legal advantage in a custody determination. The consequence of both parents having equal rights to custody is that either one can move the children to another location without directly violating any law. This may not be a wise thing to do, however. The risk in moving a child from its usual environment to another is that when a custody hearing is eventually held, the trial judge may conclude that the parent who moved the child acted contrary to the child's best interest, especially if the move was done in secret or otherwise interfered with visitation by the other parent.

It is a crime for one parent to move a child in an attempt to avoid a custody proceeding after court pleadings have been filed asking the Family Court to decide which parent should have custody. The law provides for enhanced penalties if the removal of the child is by force or threat of force, and it allows the recovery of attorneys' fees, travel expenses, and other costs. Once a custody order is issued granting either temporary or permanent custody to one parent, it is a criminal felony in South Carolina for any person, including the noncustodial parent, to take a child out of the state with an intent to violate the custody order. If the child is returned to South Carolina within seven days, the crime will be treated as a misdemeanor. The more common consequence of violating a custody order is that the Family Court will find the offending parent in contempt of court and impose a jail term of up to one year. Whether or not punishment will be imposed is in the discretion of the trial judge, and it will depend on the particular circumstances of each case.

Perhaps the greatest deterrent to child snatching is that it is becoming much less likely that child snatching will result in a permanent change of custody. Federal law prevents the courts of one state from modifying a child custody determination of another state where the Court making the original custody determination had jurisdiction under the laws of that state and it was the home state of the child on the date of the commencement of the proceedings. Federal law also makes child snatching a federal crime.

The Family Court's Role

The Family Court has exclusive jurisdiction to decide child custody disputes. It has no jurisdiction over the custody of a child who has reached 18 years of age. Such children are considered adults and they can decide for themselves where they will live, assuming they are not mentally disabled.

There is no presumption in the law that children should be awarded to either the father or the mother. There once was a strong preference in favor of awarding custody of young children to their mothers. This is referred to as the Tender Years Doctrine. The doctrine was expressly abolished by statute in 1994, therefore, the Tender Years Doctrine can no longer be considered in deciding child custody cases in South Carolina.

The Family Court will usually award one parent custody of the child and grant visitation rights to the other parent, if the parents of the child cannot agree on the terms of child custody. Typical visitation awarded by the Family Court would be every other weekend from Friday afternoon to Sunday afternoon, with a schedule of alternating holidays, birthdays, and other special events in the child's life.

If the parents of a child can agree on the terms of custody and visitation, the Family Court will usually approve whatever arrangement they work out, so long as it is not harmful to the child.

If the parents reach an agreement about child custody, the Family Court will not alter custody later on the whim of one of the parents. Rather, the person who wishes to change the custody arrangement must prove that the current situation is having a detrimental impact on the child.

Modifications of child custody and visitation are discussed in Chapter Five, including modification requests triggered by proposals to relocate the residences of children.

Types of Child Custody: Sole and Joint

"Legal custody" refers to decision-making authority with respect to children, while "physical custody" refers to the actual residential placement of children. There are two sub-categories of legal and physical custody: sole custody and joint custody.

"Sole custody" describes the most common form of custody. One parent (the custodial parent) is awarded legal and physical custody of the child and the other parent (the noncustodial parent) has visitation with the child, typically on alternating weekends, portions of holidays, and a few weeks in the summer. "Split custody" is a variation of sole custody that occurs when there is more than one child and sole custody of one or more children is awarded to one parent and sole custody of the remaining child or children is awarded to the other parent. Split custody is only awarded where there are compelling circumstances, such as a high level of conflict/hostility between children, a considerable age difference between the children, or the inability of one parent to care for all the children. A forced separation from their siblings can have a traumatic impact on children whose lives are already being disrupted by the divorce experience.

"Joint custody" (also referred to as shared parenting or coparenting) can involve joint legal custody or joint physical custody, or both. Joint physical custody is the sharing of the residential care of the child. This may or may not involve a substantially equal division of physical custody of the child, but it typically provides both parents with something more than the traditional visitation schedule awarded to noncustodial parents in sole custody situations.

An award of joint legal custody creates an expectation that the parents will share responsibility for making major decisions about the child's welfare and upbringing, including such matters as education, health care, and religious training, just as they would if the family remained intact.

An award of joint legal and physical custody creates an additional expectation that the parent with whom a child is living at any given time will make daily decisions regarding discipline, diet, maintenance, activities, emergency care, and social interactions. If parents are awarded joint legal and physical custody involving substantially equal amounts of time with the child, it is sometimes referred to as alternating custody.

The Supreme Court of South Carolina has consistently held that joint custody is usually not conducive to the best interests and welfare of children and should be ordered only under exceptional circumstances. The only situation in which it has upheld an award of joint custody over the objection of a parent was where the evidence showed that both parents had a propensity to alienate the child from the other parent, and the ability of the child to have a normal parent/child relationship with the other parent would be compromised by awarding primary custody to one parent.

If joint custody is awarded, it should not consist of brief alternating periods of day-to-day or even week-to-week. The Supreme Court of South Carolina prefers alternating joint custody in four-week intervals to be the least disruptive as possible for the child.

Notwithstanding the Supreme Court's position on joint custody, Family Court judges have awarded joint custody for many years in cases in which both parents want it and the judges are convinced that the parents are capable of cooperating sufficiently to make it work.

How Child Custody Disputes Are Resolved

Most child custody disputes are resolved by the parties, not by the Family Court. You should not ask to be awarded child custody if you know that your spouse is better suited than you to raise the children. Child custody disputes place a strain on the emotions and finances of all parties. Most Family Court judges do not want to decide child custody disputes because it is very difficult in many cases to determine which parent will do the better job of raising children in a single parent household. However, when the parties cannot reach an agreement, the Family Court will reluctantly make that decision.

Unfortunately, a dispute over child custody significantly increases the cost of litigation for both sides. A dispute over child custody will require the lawyers to spend more time on the case, and they will charge their clients for those hours. The parties must also pay the fees of a guardian *ad litem* as well as the fees of a mediator and sometimes experts such as psychologists. There is also a risk that the children will be negatively affected by becoming issues in the litigation and perhaps having to declare with which parent they prefer to live.

A "parenting plan" must be prepared in all contested child custody cases before the temporary hearing on custody. The South Carolina Supreme Court has approved a Proposed Parenting Plan form, SCCA 466. It is available at http://www.sccourts.org/forms.

➢ Mediation

South Carolina requires an early mediation conference whenever child custody or visitation is contested

Mediation gives both parties an opportunity to sit down with a neutral person called a mediator and try to work out an agreement. The idea behind mediation is that most people will be happier with agreements they make themselves than they would be with solutions that are imposed on them by a court. Mediation proponents also believe that most parents are more capable than a judge of making the best decisions about certain issues, especially custody and visitation of their children.

There is more information about mediation in Chapter Three.

➤ **Guardians** *ad litem*

When both parents ask the Family Court to award child custody to them, a guardian *ad litem* will usually be appointed to represent the children's interests during the litigation. The reasoning behind this is that neither parent can be relied on to make an impartial decision about what is in the children's best interests when they are both fighting for custody. Therefore, a guardian *ad litem* is appointed to investigate the situation and to try to determine whether the children's best interests would be served by awarding custody to one parent or the other.

The guardian *ad litem* may take the children's wishes into consideration but is not required to do so. That is, even if the children have a clear preference to live with one parent, neither the guardian nor the judge is bound by that preference.

A guardian *ad litem* is expected to maintain a confidential relationship with the children if at all possible. Thus, it is very unlikely that a guardian *ad litem* would tell you anything that your children say to the guardian in confidence. A guardian *ad litem*, however, is allowed to disclose communications with the children if the guardian believes that it would be in the children's best interests to do so or if disclosure is ordered by a judge.

A guardian *ad litem* has no power to make decisions affecting the child, other than those that relate directly to the issues involved in the litigation. Thus, a guardian *ad litem* has no authority to make decisions about issues in a child's daily life such as with whom the child should associate, what the child should eat, when the child should go to bed, how much time the child should spend doing homework, whether to go to church or school, etc. The guardian's authority is limited to the narrow tasks of protecting the child's interests in the litigation and helping the Family Court decide which parent should be awarded custody.

If the mother and father can agree on a person who is willing to serve as the child's guardian *ad litem*, the Family Court will likely accept the parents' recommendation. More commonly, the Family Court will appoint someone unknown to the parties. This may be a lawyer, although a person does not have to be a lawyer to serve as a guardian *ad litem*. Even if the Court appoints a lawyer to serve as the guardian *ad litem*, however, that person will function as a guardian *ad litem*, not as a lawyer for the child. In some instances, a guardian *ad litem* who is not a lawyer may ask the Family Court to appoint a lawyer to represent the guardian, for example, when complex issues of law exist or a guardian anticipates needing to call witnesses at the final hearing.

The parents are normally expected to split payment of the guardian's fee unless the Family Court determines that one parent should pay more than half or all of it. The guardian's fee must be approved by the Family Court based on an itemized billing statement.

The guardian *ad litem*'s job is frequently quite difficult, particularly in cases where both parents are fit to have custody. The guardian's ultimate objective is to determine whether there are reasons to believe that one parent would do a better job as the custodial parent than the other parent. This requires a diligent guardian *ad litem* to investigate virtually every aspect of the child's life. As an agent of the Family Court, the guardian *ad litem* has broad powers of investigation and is entitled to have access to any records that might be relevant to the custody decision. The guardian will typically meet with the child and with each parent, both privately and in the presence of the child. The guardian may also talk to neighbors, other relatives, teachers, doctors, or anyone else who may have relevant information. The guardian should examine the child's school records and visit both parents' homes.

As a parent involved in a child custody dispute, you should be on your best behavior in the presence of the guardian *ad litem* and do everything possible to make the guardian's job easier rather than more difficult. You should answer the guardian's questions honestly, even if you think it might put you in a bad light. You do not want to take a risk that the guardian *ad litem* will discover that you were dishonest, for this would almost certainly affect the guardian's report and the judge's decision.

Try to resist saying negative things about your spouse, unless it involves something that clearly affects his or her ability or fitness to raise the child and unless you have some independent proof that what you are saying is true (documents, pictures, or witnesses for example). Custody is often awarded to the parent who seems to be the more willing parent to foster a positive relationship between the child and the other parent. Parents who unnecessarily criticize their spouses are not helping themselves win the custody battle.

However, if you think the guardian is being too intrusive into your life or that of your child or is otherwise not discharging his or her duties responsibly, you should express your concerns to your lawyer. You should be especially observant for any signs that meetings or telephone conversations with the guardian *ad litem* are upsetting your child.

The guardian *ad litem* is expected to submit a written report to the Court and to the lawyers for both spouses prior to the final court hearing on child custody (this is usually part of the final hearing in divorce cases or other marital litigation). The report should not recommend which parent should have custody. The report will describe the information obtained through the guardian's investigation. At the court hearing, the lawyers for the husband and the wife will present testimony of witnesses, and they are allowed to cross examine the guardian and anyone who provided information to the guardian.

The trial judge will decide custody based on the evidence submitted by the guardian, the husband, and the wife at the final hearing. Sometimes, both parents will appear equally suited to have primary custody of the child. This makes the judge's decision a very difficult one.

The guardian *ad litem*'s term of appointment generally ends when the final order is filed, unless the custody decision is appealed.

➤ Best Interests of Children is the Governing Factor

No area of law seems to operate under a single standard more than child custody. All jurisdictions recognize the principle that the best interest of the children is the controlling factor in custody cases. Even though this area of the law is nominally governed by a single principle, it is muddled by difficulty of definition and explanation. The difficulty is in applying the best interests standard to the facts of the case. A determination of what is in the best interests of a child requires consideration of all of the circumstances of the particular case and usually many factors.

The concept of "best interests" is open to many interpretations and often used in divorce litigation to support the positions of both parents simultaneously. This results in inconsistent custody decisions that may or may not serve the best interests of children. A useful working definition of "best interests" is "what combination of factors this child needs in a custody and/or access arrangement that will sustain his or her adjustment or development."

There is universal agreement among social scientists that children's interests are best served by being raised by both parents in an intact, loving family. Maintaining the stability of the family unit and the continuity of healthy relationships within it is the surest way to advance the best interests of a child. Following divorce, the best way to foster a child's development is to maintain the closest semblance possible to the lifestyle and family relationships that existed during the marriage.

Unfortunately, this ideal post-divorce circumstance is not and cannot be realized in most post-divorce situations. A joint custody plan cannot be imposed successfully upon parents who do not want it or who are not capable of making it work. Some parents cannot cooperate due to a history of conflict or for other reasons. In most post-divorce situations, parents drift apart, establish new relationships, and begin new families.

The relationships between parents and among parents and their children inevitably change following divorce, particularly the relationships among noncustodial parents and their children. The relationship between the parents and the children is necessarily different after a divorce and, accordingly, it may be unrealistic in some cases to try to preserve the noncustodial parent's accustomed close involvement in the children's everyday lives at the expense of the custodial parent's efforts to start a new life or to form a new family unit.

Another problem with the movement toward joint custody is that many joint custody arrangements turn out to be joint custody in name only, not true shared parenting relationships where both parents continue taking responsibility for parenting the children. One scholar complained that joint custody arrangements too often did little more than add rights, rather than responsibilities, which interfered with the ability of the true custodial parent to raise the child properly.

There are some exceptions to the general rule in which exceptionally committed and cooperative parents are able to maintain a reasonable semblance of the original family unit, including the continuance of familial relationships that closely resemble those that existed prior to the divorce. This is the optimal, though rare, post-divorce environment. When it exists, courts are often willing to give parents an opportunity to try to make joint custody work for the child, but only if they request it and only if they present a parenting plan in which both parents have parenting responsibilities, not just expanded rights.

Courts review requests for joint custody cautiously, however, to ensure that it is not being requested by a parent as a strategy for reducing his or her child support obligation or for any other improper motive. Courts are sometimes tempted to permit or impose joint custody simply to avoid making a difficult choice between two fit parents. Studies establish that yielding to this temptation is not likely to produce a workable agreement nor is it in the best interests of children.

> **Specific Factors Used to Determine the Best Interests of Children**

When the Family Court is asked to decide which parent will have custody, it will consider all factors that might relate to the fitness of a parent or the best interests of a child. Seldom is any one factor determinative of the outcome. Most cases involve consideration of a wide range of topics, including: who has been the primary caretaker;

the conduct, attributes, and fitness of the parents; the opinions of third parties (including the guardian, expert witnesses, and the children); and the age, health, and sex of the children.

The Family Court, by its own review of the evidence, will consider the character, fitness, attitude, and inclinations on the part of each parent as they impact the child as well as all psychological, physical, environmental, spiritual, educational, medical, family, emotional, and recreational aspects of the child's life. When determining to whom custody should be awarded, the Family Court will consider all the circumstances of the particular case and all relevant factors must be taken into consideration. In sum, a determination of the best interests of a child will depend on the particular facts of each case.

The relative fitness of the parents to raise a child is often the determining factor in child custody disputes. Fitness decisions frequently focus on two considerations: whether either parent has been the primary caretaker, or whether either parent has engaged or is likely to engage in conduct that would harm the welfare of the child.

Custody will almost always be awarded to a parent who has clearly been the **primary caretaker of the child**, unless the unfitness of that parent is proved or there is other compelling evidence that the welfare of a child will be better served by awarding custody to the other parent. In modern society, however, it is common for both parents to work, thus making it difficult to identify either one as the primary caretaker.

A custody decision can be based on a Family Court judge's conclusion that a parent has engaged in **conduct that is detrimental to a child**. Detrimental conduct includes refusing to let the other parent visit the child, falsely accusing the other parent of misconduct such as child abuse, making negative statements about the other parent to the child, acting irresponsibly with the family's finances, engaging in an Internet affair, not controlling one's temper, allowing the child to be absent or excessively tardy getting to school or otherwise neglecting the child's education, and missing activities in which the child is engaged.

Cases involving questions of unfitness commonly focus on parental conduct that is considered "immoral," but a custody decision should not turn on this factor unless there is some connection between the parent's conduct and the welfare of the child. **The morality of a parent** is a proper consideration in determining child custody but it is limited in its force to what relevancy it has, either indirectly or directly, to the welfare of the child. For example, the South Carolina Court of Appeals in 1999 upheld a Family Court ruling that there was no evidence that a mother's job as a topless dancer adversely affected her ability to parent the parties' two children. The Court of Appeals said that "[a]bsent such evidence, Mother's occupation is not a relevant consideration in denying her custody." The Court acknowledged that some people may consider the mother's occupation, though legal, immoral, but it concluded that the effect that a parent's morality may have on his or her fitness to have custody is limited to what relevancy it has, either directly or indirectly, to the welfare of the child. Another case held that the existence of a criminal record including time in prison does not automatically render a parent unfit to have custody of a child.

Examples of immoral conduct that have made a difference in custody decisions include exposing children to adulterous relationships, having a promiscuous or bohemian lifestyle, using drugs, excessive consumption of alcohol, emotional instability, current psychiatric care, and attempted suicide.

Immoral conduct is less likely to be relevant to a custody decision if the trial judge is convinced that the conduct has ended and the moral lapse is not likely to be repeated.

Homosexual conduct does not render a person unfit to have custody as a matter of law, but it may affect a custody decision if the child is exposed to homosexual acts or if the homosexual lifestyle of the parent is otherwise proved to have a detrimental impact on the child.

The Family Court is specifically directed to consider evidence of **domestic violence** in making child custody decisions and not to use the fact that a victim of domestic violence left the marital home as a reason for denying custody.

A separate issue from the fitness of the parents is **the attributes and resources of each parent**, that is, what each parent will be able to provide for children who are placed in his or her custody. This can involve a wide range of issues, such as financial and physical resources, free time to spend with the children, access to friends and relatives, the availability of child care, tenderness, caring, and religious training. While parents who can stay home and care for children are preferred for custody if other considerations are relatively equal, the need to place a child in daycare will not defeat a parent's claim for custody if there are more serious problems in the other parent's home. The education and parenting skills of a parent are legitimate factors to consider. Further, the special attention necessitated by learning difficulties or poor performance in school are considerations to be taken into account in deciding which parent should have custody.

The Family Court may take into consideration **the preferences of the children**. Although South Carolina law does not recognize a certain age when children have a right to select the custodial parent, the Family Court will ordinarily give great weight to the wishes of children once they are between 12 and 14 years old, depending on their maturity. Absent evidence tending to establish that the best interests of older children would be served by awarding custody to the other parent, the Court will let older children live with whichever parent they prefer. The Court may consider the wishes of children of any age, but South Carolina courts have given little significance to the wishes of six-year-old or younger children. The primary question for the Family Court is what is best for the welfare of the children.

The **opinions of guardians** *ad litem* **and other expert witnesses** play an increasingly important role in child custody disputes. The presumable objectivity of these participants, especially guardians *ad litem* or experts appointed by the Court, makes them highly influential to the trial judge. The Family Court may also consider the suggestions of social service agencies and medical professionals.

Custody Disputes Between a Biological Parent and a Third Party

There is a presumption in favor of awarding custody to the biological parent when a biological parent (mother or father) becomes involved in a custody dispute with a third party, whether it is a relative such as a grandparent or a nonrelative such as a foster parent. One case in South Carolina says that "[o]nce the natural parent is deemed fit, the issue of custody is decided." This strong preference only applies to disputes between a biological parent and a third party, not to disputes between third parties and other relatives of the child.

In extremely compelling circumstances, a "psychological parent" can be awarded custody even over the objections of the biological parent. A statute enacted in 2006 allows the Family Court to award custody to "de facto parents," third parties who have been the primary caretakers of children for specified periods of time, if the natural parents are unfit or other compelling circumstances exist.

The presumption in favor of the biological parent is not quite as strong in situations in which the biological parents voluntarily relinquish custody to some other person, then change their minds and seek to resume custody of the child. In such situations, the Family

Court must consider three factors in addition to the fitness of the biological parents: (1) the amount of contact, as measured by visitation, financial support, or both, that the parents had with the child while in the care of a third party; (2) the circumstances under which the temporary relinquishment occurred; and (3) the degree of attachment between the child and the temporary custodian. The child has been returned to the biological parents in most cases that have considered these factors.

Interstate Child Custody Disputes

The Family Court of South Carolina may not have jurisdiction to decide a child custody dispute if the parents do not both live in South Carolina or if the child whose custody is in dispute has lived in South Carolina for less than six months. Whether South Carolina has jurisdiction either to make an award of child custody or to modify an existing child custody order from another state depends on an analysis of the circumstances.

Federal law requires a two-step analysis under most circumstances. First, the Court must determine whether it has jurisdiction. Second, the Court must determine whether it is proper to exercise its jurisdiction.

Whether jurisdiction exists to make a child custody determination by initial or modification decree depends on whether the Family Court of South Carolina has jurisdiction under the laws of South Carolina, and one of the following conditions is met:

1. South Carolina is the home state of the child on the date of the commencement of the proceeding, or had been the child's home state within six months before the date of the commencement of the proceeding and the child is absent

from such state because of his removal or retention by a contestant or for other reasons, and a contestant continues to live in such state; or

2. It appears that no other state would have jurisdiction as the child's home state, and it is in the best interest of the child for a court of South Carolina to assume jurisdiction because the child and his parents, or the child and at least one contestant, have a significant connection with South Carolina other than mere physical presence in South Carolina, and there is available in South Carolina substantial evidence concerning the child's present or future care, protection, training, and personal relationships; or

3 The child is physically present in South Carolina and the child has been abandoned, or it is necessary in an emergency to protect the child because he has been subjected to or threatened with mistreatment or abuse; or

4. It appears that no other state would have jurisdiction, or another state has declined to exercise jurisdiction on the ground that South Carolina is the more appropriate forum to determine the custody of the child, and it is in the best interest of the child that South Carolina assume jurisdiction; or

5. The Court has continuing jurisdiction over the matter.

Thus, jurisdictional priority goes to the "home state" of the child. Once a state is the "home state," it remains the "home state" for six months after the child leaves if a contestant remains there. Inquiry into "significant connections" or "substantial evidence" is only to be made when there is no "home state" or no other state has jurisdiction otherwise.

Federal Law provides that once a court makes a child custody determination, it has continuing jurisdiction as long as it continues to have jurisdiction under the laws of its state and the child or any contestant continues to live there.

State and federal law restrict the ability of one state's courts to modify the custody decrees of another state's courts. One state can modify a child custody decree of another state, only if (1) it has jurisdiction to make such a child custody determination; and (2) the court of the other state no longer has jurisdiction, or it has declined to exercise its jurisdiction.

The issue of whether South Carolina should exercise jurisdiction usually centers on whether South Carolina is an inconvenient forum. A judge faced with this issue must consider among other things whether: (1) another state recently was the child's home state; (2) another state has closer connection with the child and his family; and (3) if substantial evidence concerning the child's present or future care, protection, training and personal relationships is more readily available in another state.

The trial court can award attorneys' fees and litigation expenses to defendants in child custody cases if jurisdiction is declined because the person requesting custody wrongfully took the child from another state or engaged in similar reprehensible conduct. Attorneys' fees and costs can also be awarded to people who incur expenses enforcing other states' custody orders in South Carolina.

Child custody orders from other states can be registered in South Carolina for enforcement purposes. The application form for registering an out-of-state child custody order, SCCA 458A, is located at http://www.sccourts.org/forms.

Visitation

Where the custody of a minor child is awarded to one parent by a divorce decree, it is the prevailing practice to grant visitation rights to the parent who does not have custody. The Family Court has the power to deny visitation rights when the circumstances justify doing so, however, the estrangement of child and parent should be avoided whenever possible. In determining whether the parent who does not have custody should be given visitation rights, the welfare and best interests of the child are the primary considerations.

The question of determining and limiting visitation rights is one addressed to the broad discretion of the trial judge and in the absence of a clear abuse of discretion, the order granting, denying, or limiting visitation rights will not be disturbed. However, a judicial award of the custody of a child and the fixing of visitation rights is not final and changed circumstances may authorize a change of custody or visitation rights in the future.

The general rule is that minor children, notwithstanding the divorce, are entitled to the love and companionship of both parents, and the well-rounded development of a normal child demands an association with both parents. However, if a parent has committed domestic violence, the Family Court may award that parent visitation rights only if the Court finds that the safety of the child and the victim of domestic violence can be protected. Courts may prohibit visitation altogether by people who commit domestic violence or they may impose specific restrictions on visitation to protect children and victims of physical violence. Courts are also authorized to order people who commit domestic violence to pay the costs of supervised visitation, post bonds for the return and safety of children, and pay for medical and psychological treatment of children who are affected by domestic violence.

South Carolina appellate courts have consistently held that there is no relationship between visitation rights and child support payments. A custodial parent cannot withhold visitation because of a noncustodial parent's failure to make child support payments. Even if the custodial parent improperly prevents visitation, child support payments must continue to be made.

The custodial parent is not required to pay child support to the noncustodial parent when the child is visiting the noncustodial parent. The fixed obligation of a custodial parent to provide for the necessities of life for the children is a continuing one and does not cease during the temporary absences of the children while on visitation. Courts have held that it is against the weight of reason to require the custodial parent to pay child support to the noncustodial parent during temporary periods of visitation, in addition to maintaining at all times a permanent home for the children. Likewise, the noncustodial parent remains obligated to pay child support even during times of extended visitation, absent a court order to the contrary.

Each parent, whether the custodial or noncustodial parent of the child, has equal access and the same right to obtain all educational records and medical records of his or her minor children.

➤ Terms and Conditions of Visitation

Courts do not get involved in setting terms or conditions of child visitation unless they are asked to do so. First, they lack subject matter jurisdiction until a litigant puts visitation in issue. Second, most judges prefer for the parties to work out suitable arrangements between themselves. It is very difficult to set visitation terms and conditions that will suit both parents for as long as their children are minors.

The custodial parent has the inherent authority to set terms and conditions of visitation when children are temporarily in the custody of other people, such as baby sitters, school officials, and others with whom the children spend the night or travel. It is less clear to what extent the custodial parent is permitted to set terms and conditions of visitation when the children are temporarily in the care of the noncustodial parent, but the most likely rule is that the custodial parent cannot dictate rules about visitation to the noncustodial parent absent unusual circumstances.

The Family Courts will impose restrictions on visitation beyond those normally imposed on noncustodial parents if they are reasonable and necessary to protect the welfare of the child. The privilege of visitation must yield to the best interests of the children and may be denied or limited if the best interests of the children will be served.

Restricted or supervised visitation may be ordered where one of the parents is involving the child in disputes with the custodial parent. A child's need to attend Sunday School or, presumably, to participate in other scheduled activities does not justify placing extraordinary limits on the noncustodial parent's visitation rights.

The Family Court has continuing jurisdiction to modify the terms and conditions of visitation if a showing is made that the best interests of the child will be served by modifying visitation rights, but the Family Court may not modify visitation unless such relief is specifically requested in the pleadings.

The Family Court may terminate or suspend the visitation privileges of a parent if it is in the child's best interests, although a decision to prevent visitation totally between a parent and a child is a drastic one that Family Court judges will make only in cases involving serious misbehavior. For example, visitation may be denied when a parent sexually abuses or otherwise is a threat to the safety of the child, or where the noncustodial parent engages in other conduct that makes visitation harmful to the child physically or emotionally. In one case, for example, the visitation rights of the father were suspended where he made derogatory comments about the mother in the child's presence, he parked near her home and lurked about, he followed the mother and child to and from work and school blowing his horn and maneuvering around her vehicle, and he and other members of his family tried to get the child to lie about his mother so the father could obtain custody.

➢ **Siblings Visitation**

When brothers and sisters are not living together, the Family Court can order sibling visitation when it finds that it would be in the siblings' best interests.

➢ **Grandparents Visitation**

Grandparents are not entitled to court-ordered visitation if their grandchild's parents are living together. Otherwise, they may seek visitation in limited circumstances.

It is a generally accepted principle of law that a child's parents who are living together with the child can decide who will be allowed to spend time with the child, and they can lawfully prevent a minor child from associating with anyone whom they choose to exclude from the child's life, including the child's grandparents.

Grandparents usually have no right to seek visitation if the Family Court has terminated the parental rights of their grandchildrens' parents, for example during an adoption proceeding.

The Family Court cannot require fit parents to justify their refusal to allow grandparent visitation, and there must be compelling circumstances, such as significant harm to the child that would be caused by denying visitation, to overcome the presumption that such decisions by fit parents are in their child's best interest.

The South Carolina Supreme Court has recognized in its opinions that a decision of the U.S. Supreme Court requires Family Courts to give "special weight" to a fit parent's decision regarding visitation. The U.S. Supreme Court wrote that "[s]o long as a parent adequately cares for his or her children (*i.e.*, is fit), there will normally be no reason for the State to inject itself into the private realm of the family to further question the ability of that parent to make the best decisions concerning the rearing of that parent's children." Parental unfitness must be shown by clear and convincing evidence. The presumption that a fit parent's decision is in the best interest of the child may be overcome only by showing compelling circumstances, such as significant harm to the child if visitation is not granted. The fact that a child may benefit from contact with the grandparent, or that the parent's refusal is simply not reasonable in the court's view, does not justify governmental interference in the parent's decision.

If their grandchild's parents are not living together, grandparents have standing to seek court-ordered visitation with a grandchild when one of the following situations exists:

- either or both parents of a minor child are dead;

- the parents are divorced; or

- the parents are living separate and apart in different habitats regardless of a court order or agreement.

If one or both of the grandchild's parents are alive, visitation cannot be awarded to grandparents unless the Family Court finds that it would not interfere with the parent-child relationship.

➤ Stepparents and Others Visitation

Stepparents normally do not have a right to seek court-ordered visitation with their stepchildren in South Carolina.

In compelling circumstances, however, a "psychological parent" can be awarded visitation even over the objections of the biological parents. In order to demonstrate the existence of a psychological parent-child relationship, the petitioner must show:

(1)   that the biological or adoptive parent[s] consented to, and fostered, the petitioner's formation and establishment of a parent-like relationship with the child;

(2)   that the petitioner and the child lived together in the same household;

(3)   that the petitioner assumed obligations of parenthood by taking significant responsibility for the child's care, education and development, including contributing towards the child's support, without expectation of financial compensation; and

(4)   that the petitioner has been in a parental role for a length of time sufficient to have established with the child a bonded, dependent relationship parental in nature.

The Family Court can also award visitation to "de facto parents" (third parties who have been the primary caretakers of children for specified periods of time) if the natural parents are unfit or other compelling circumstances exist.

Child Support

In General

Mothers and fathers are required by law to support all of their minor children, whether the children were born during marriage or out of wedlock. A father is not responsible after divorce for the support of his wife's illegitimate child by another man who was born before the marriage, unless he formally adopts the child. A husband who consents for his wife to conceive a child through artificial insemination with the understanding that the child will be treated as his own is the legal father of the child and will be charged with all of the legal responsibilities of paternity, including support.

The fact that one parent has not requested child support from the other parent is not an excuse for failing to provide support for a child. If a parent does not provide adequate child support, he or she can be ordered to do so at any time, and the Family Court can order the parent to pay retroactive child support to make up for previous inadequacies. In theory, a parent can be forced to pay retroactive child support from the time he or she stopped providing adequate support for the child, or at least from the time the parent stopped living with the child. Even though a child has reached 18, the custodial parent or the child may still be able to obtain child support from the other parent for the period before the child reached the age of majority. The chances of obtaining retroactive child support diminish with time, however, so the sooner one pursues child support, the more likely it is that the Family Court will award retroactive support.

The Family Court may also award retroactive child support if the Court finds that the supporting parent failed to disclose income or assets at the time of the initial support award. This is to prevent manifest injustice and possible condonation of a fraud perpetrated upon the Court.

Any transfer of income or property for the purpose of avoiding a child support obligation is "clearly and utterly void."

Enforcement and modification of child support is discussed in Chapter Five.

Establishing Paternity and Support Obligations

The issue of paternity (who is the father?) is sometimes the threshold question in actions for child support. Children born during the course of a marriage are presumed to be the children of the husband and wife of that marriage. If there is any question about the paternity of a child, the Family Court can order a person who is alleged to be the parent of a child to submit to a simple, inexpensive genetic testing procedure that will determine whether or not he is the parent of the child.

It is extremely important for husbands involved in divorce proceedings to consider carefully whether there is any chance they are not the biological fathers of their children. If the divorce pleadings allege that children were born of the marriage, and this factual allegation is not challenged during the divorce proceeding, the final decree of divorce serves as an adjudication of paternity, and it cannot be challenged later. A husband cannot rely on his wife's representations that the children are his. He has an independent obligation to inquire (*i.e.*, to seek paternity testing), or he will be responsible for supporting the children at least until they reach 18 years of age, even if he finds out later that the mother intentionally misled him and that someone else is actually the father.

It is becoming less frequent for private lawyers to be involved in establishing paternity or in establishing or enforcing child support. This is a result of the creation of an administrative process for establishing and enforcing paternity and child support and the existence of powerful enforcement tools that are available only to the Child Support Enforcement Division of the Department of Social Services (the Division).

A new era in child support law began in South Carolina in 1990 when the South Carolina Child Support Guidelines became effective. Previously, child support awards in South Carolina were determined on a case-by-case basis, and there were no standard criteria for making such determinations. The promulgation of the Guidelines coincided with aggressive federal initiatives to force states to get tough on nonsupporting parents. The ultimate goal of federal activities in the area of child support enforcement is to make the payment of child support automatic and inescapable.

The Child Support Enforcement Division of the Department of Social Services (the Division) establishes paternity and establishes and enforces child support orders for individuals receiving its services. Any person can receive assistance from the Division by completing and submitting an application form and paying a nominal fee irrespective of his or her income. The services of the Division are available to both custodial and noncustodial parents. A person may request the Division's full services or may just request a specific service such as assistance in locating an absent parent (the Division has access to numerous federal, interstate, state, and local sources to locate absent parents).

Information about the services that are provided by the Division, including answers to frequently asked questions, is on the DSS Child Support Services website at www.state.sc.us/dss/csed. The telephone number is 800-768-5858.

Before the 1990's, filing an action in the Family Court was the only way to establish the paternity and child support obligation of a parent. This was often time consuming and expensive. Today, a more efficient administrative process provides an alternative to court proceedings.

The Administrative Process for Establishing and Enforcing Paternity and Child Support begins with a notice of financial responsibility from the Child Support Enforcement Division to an alleged father. The notice informs the father of the allegation of paternity and provides additional information, including the right to request a court hearing. An alleged father has 30 days to object to the notice of financial responsibility and make a written request for a court hearing. If no request is made for a court hearing, the alleged father can be required to attend a "negotiation conference" with the Division to discuss the allegation of paternity.

If an alleged father fails to attend the negotiation conference and does not make a timely written denial of paternity, the Division may enter an order declaring the alleged father to be the legal father of the child. This order takes effect in 15 days unless the alleged father shows good cause for missing the negotiation conference or not filing a written denial of paternity. There is no requirement that a default order declaring paternity be approved by a Family Court judge, but a default order setting child support must be approved by a Family Court judge.

If an alleged father attends the negotiation conference and admits paternity, the Division can issue a consent order finding that the person is the father of the child and setting an agreed upon amount of child support (the amount must be consistent with the Child Support Guidelines). The consent order does not have to be approved by a Family Court judge. When the order is filed with the appropriate clerk of court, it has all the force, effect, and remedies of an order of the Family Court.

If an alleged parent attends the negotiation conference but denies paternity, the Division can issue a subpoena ordering the alleged parent to submit to paternity genetic testing, if the testimony and supplementary evidence presented at the negotiation conference demonstrate a reasonable probability that the alleged father had sexual intercourse with the child's mother during the probable time of the child's conception or if the evidence shows a probable existence of a presumption. A reasonable probability of sexual intercourse during the possible time of conception may be established by an affidavit of the child's mother.

The Division may apply to the Family Court for an order compelling an alleged parent to submit to genetic testing. The Family Court must enter the order compelling the alleged parent to submit to genetic testing if the Court finds reasonable cause to believe that the alleged father is the natural or presumed father of the child.

The Family Court has the power upon its own motion or that of any "interested party" to order the mother, the child, and the alleged father to undergo genetic tests. The Court may also order any male witness who offers testimony indicating that his act of intercourse with the natural mother may have resulted in the conception of the child to undergo genetic testing or other tests to determine whether he is the child's father.

Results of genetic tests or the refusal of a party to submit to such tests are admissible at a paternity hearing as are voluntary acknowledgments of paternity, foreign paternity determinations, and paternity indicated on birth certificates.

Duration of Child Support Obligation

A parent's obligation to provide "reasonable support" for a child usually ends when the child reaches 18 years of age, unless: (1) the child becomes emancipated sooner; (2) special circumstances exist that justify requiring parents to continue providing support for their children; or (3) the parents agree to continue providing support. Child support payments are ordinarily terminated by the death of the child or the party making the payments.

Whether a child is emancipated depends upon the facts and circumstances of each case. Emancipation during minority results not from any act of the child alone, but primarily from agreement of the parents, which may be either express or implied. Emancipation of a minor child is never presumed, and the burden of proof is upon the person who alleges it.

The fact that one of several children has reached majority does not affect a parent's child support obligation, absent a Family Court order modifying the amount of support owed. However, when child support is terminated due to the child turning 18 years of age, graduating from high school, or reaching the end of the school year when the child is 19, no arrearage may be incurred as to that child after the date of the child's 18th birthday, the date of the child's graduation from high school, or the last day of the school year when the child is 19, whichever date terminated the child support obligation.

The Family Court may order parents to provide support past age 18 where there are physical or mental disabilities of the child that warrant the continuation of child support beyond age 18 for as long as the physical or mental disabilities continue. The language in the statute that provides for this appears to reflect a clear legislative choice that, between parents and society as a whole, it is preferable for parents to be charged with the long-term support obligation for physically or mentally disabled children, at least to the extent that they are able to undertake it. However, a learning disabled child may not be entitled to child support after reaching majority if he can work and make financial contributions to his own support.

Parents have also been ordered by the Family Court to support a child who is over 18 years of age where the child became sick, injured, or otherwise disabled shortly after becoming emancipated.

The Family Court has the authority to include in a support order "the expense of educating his or her child." Parents are required to provide support for their unemancipated children in high school, even after they reach 18 years of age. The propriety of ordering parents to pay private schooling expenses for children under 18 is not yet completely settled. Parents have been ordered to pay for private schools for children under 18 when special circumstances show the need for it. A parent might be required to pay for private school if the Court determines that it would be in the best interests of the child to attend a private school, even absent special circumstances.

Parents who are separated or divorced may be required by a Family Court judge to contribute enough money to enable a child over 18 to attend four years of college where there is evidence that: (1) the characteristics of the child indicate that he or she will benefit from college; (2) the child demonstrates the ability to do well, or at least to make satisfactory grades; (3) the child cannot otherwise go to school; and (4) the parent has the financial ability to help to pay for such an education. It is not yet clear in South Carolina whether children must first exhaust other avenues of raising money for college before their parents will be ordered to help them. Some court decisions indicate that a child must pursue available scholarships and jobs to help defray the costs of education, but the Supreme Court of South Carolina has not yet ruled on this issue.

Effect of Agreements Regarding Support

The Family Court will ordinarily enforce agreements in which parents promise to provide more support than the Child Support Guidelines would require, but not agreements that allow parents to pay less. Agreements that purport to release a parent from child support obligations are not binding on the Family Court.

In matters affecting the welfare of children, the Family Court's authority cannot be limited by any agreement between the parents. The Family Court has continuing jurisdiction to do whatever is in the best interests of the child regardless of what an agreement between the parents specifies. The Family Court has jurisdiction to determine what is in the best interests of the children, and an agreement entered into upon divorce cannot prejudice the rights of children. If parents agree to an amount of child support and ask the Family Court to approve it, the judge must determine whether it is reasonable and in the best interests of the child.

Amount of Child Support

The amount of support depends on the parents' income and assets or their ability to earn the means to provide child support. The primary factors considered under the Guidelines are the actual gross incomes and earning potential of both parents. However, the Family Court is required to consider additional factors, including the parents' ability to pay; their education, expenses, and assets; and the facts and circumstances surrounding each case. The Court's objective is to award support in an amount sufficient to provide for the needs of the children and to maintain the children at the standard of living they would have been provided but for the divorce. The award should be an amount the parent can pay and still meet his or her own needs.

Since 1990, the amount of child support to be awarded is based on the South Carolina Child Support Guidelines, unless the Family Court makes a specific finding that application of the Guidelines would be unjust or inappropriate. When the parents' combined incomes are so high that the Guidelines do not cover the case, the amount of child support should reflect that a child is entitled to live and be supported in a life style commensurate with the current income of his parents.

The Child Support Guidelines establish minimum contributions that must be applied by the courts in determining the amount that an absent parent is expected to pay toward the support of a dependent child. The Guidelines rely primarily on the incomes of both parents in calculating child support awards. Income is defined to include the actual gross income of the parent, if employed to full capacity, or potential income if unemployed or underemployed. Gross income includes income from any source including salaries, wages, commissions, royalties, bonuses, rents (less allowable business expenses), dividends, severance pay, pensions, interest, trust income, annuities, capital gains, social security benefits (but not Supplemental Security Income), worker's compensation benefits, unemployment insurance benefits, disability insurance benefits, Veteran's benefits and alimony, including alimony that a party received as a result of another marriage and alimony that a party receives as a result of the current litigation. Unreported cash income should also be included if it can be identified.

The Court may also take into account assets available to generate income for child support. For example, the Court may determine the reasonable earning potential of any asset at its market value and assess against it the current treasury bill interest rate or some other similar appropriate method of computing income. In addition to determining potential earnings, the Court should impute income to any non-income producing assets of either parent, if significant, other than a primary residence or personal property.

Examples of such assets are vacation homes (if not maintained as rental property) and idle land. The current rate determined by the Court is the rate at which income should be imputed to such non-performing assets.

If a parent is unemployed or underemployed, that parent's potential or prospective income should be considered. However, the Court may take into account the presence of young children or handicapped children who must be cared for by the parent, necessitating the parent's inability to work.

Since 1999, the Guidelines give credit for other children for whom parents are required to pay support, including additional natural or adopted children living in the home, but not for step-children unless a court order establishes a legal responsibility.

The Guidelines include separate worksheets for calculating child support where the parents split or share custody. Split custody refers to custody arrangements where there are two or more children and each parent has physical custody of at least one child. The objective of the Guidelines is to apportion fairly between the parents the total child support needed for all the children and to allocate it so that each child has access to the same amount of child support.

Where parents share custody of the same child or children, the Guidelines seek to fairly apportion child support based on the percentage of time that the child is living with each parent, based on a belief that the noncustodial parent's expenses will be increased in a true shared custody arrangement. Of course, any reduction in the amount of child support paid by the noncustodial parent is also a reduction in the amount of child support received by the custodial parent.

The shared parenting adjustment first appeared in the Guidelines in 1999, and it immediately raised concerns among practicing lawyers about its potential for producing inequitable results and increased litigation. The primary concern about the shared parenting adjustment is that the amount of visitation needed to qualify for using the worksheet is not very much more than the standard visitation typically awarded to noncustodial parents, yet, the use of the shared parenting worksheet can have a significant impact on the amount of child support being received by the custodial parent.

The shared parenting worksheet can only be used with Court approval. Where the amount of visitation meets the shared parenting threshold, child support should be calculated using both worksheets before deciding whether to use it. In some cases, the shared parenting worksheet may produce unfair results to the custodial parent by significantly reducing child support, and in other cases, it may produce unfair results to the noncustodial parent because there are some situations in which the shared parenting worksheet will actually increase the amount of child support owed to the custodial parent.

Copies of the Child Support Guidelines and the worksheets for calculating child support can be obtained from the DSS Child Support Services office at 800-768-5858. The Guidelines can also be accessed online at www.state.sc.us/dss/csed. A child support calculator tool is also located on the website.

Tax Consequences

Child support payments are not deductible from the payer's income nor taxed as income to the person receiving the payments if (1) they are fixed by a court order or agreement at the time the payments are made and (2) the payments are for the support of children of the payer.

The custodial parent (divorced or separated) is entitled to the dependency exemption so long as both parties contribute at least half of the child's support. This right can be assigned to the noncustodial parent either by agreement or by order of the Family Court. If a support award is not allocated between spousal and child support, the amount is taxable to the supported spouse and non-taxable to the supporting spouse.

Paternity and Child Support Disputes Between Parents Who Do Not Both Live in South Carolina

A broad long arm jurisdiction statute allows South Carolina to obtain personal jurisdiction over nonresidents in child support and paternity proceedings. South Carolina courts can exercise personal jurisdiction over a nonresident in a proceeding to establish, enforce, or modify a support order or to determine parentage under a range of circumstances. These include whether the individual ever resided with the child in South Carolina or if the individual ever engaged in sexual intercourse in South Carolina and the child may have been conceived by that act of intercourse.

If personal jurisdiction cannot be obtained over an out-of-state parent by using the long arm jurisdiction statute, the Uniform Interstate Family Support Act (UIFSA) can be used to establish and enforce support obligations when a party defendant lives outside of South Carolina. Although a person may choose to hire a private lawyer to pursue child support, it is not necessary. UIFSA provides a mechanism whereby the Child Support Enforcement Division of the Department of Social Services can represent the interests of an individual seeking to establish or enforce a support obligation.

UIFSA applies to the establishment and enforcement of paternity and spousal and child support obligations and to the modification of child support. UIFSA proceedings may be used when a resident or agency of South Carolina wants to establish or enforce the support obligation of a person who lives in another state, in which case a South Carolina tribunal is the "initiating tribunal." UIFSA can also be used when a nonresident or a child support enforcement agency of another state wants to establish or enforce the support obligation of a South Carolina resident, in which case a South Carolina tribunal is the "responding tribunal."

A custodial parent who lives in South Carolina is not required to go to the state where the other parent lives for the establishment, enforcement, or modification of a support order or the determination of parentage. Special rules of evidence allow the verified petition and verified testimony of the custodial parent to be admitted into evidence without the custodial parent being present. Special discovery rules also permit a tribunal to: (1) communicate with a tribunal of another state in writing, by telephone, or otherwise to obtain information concerning the laws of that state, the legal effects of judgments, decrees, or orders, and the status of proceedings there; (2) request a tribunal of another state to assist in discovery; and (3) compel a person over whom it has jurisdiction to respond to discovery issued by a tribunal of another state.

An alternative procedure for enforcing existing support and income withholding orders is provided in UIFSA. A party may register for enforcement purposes another state's support order, income withholding order, or both, by sending the documents required for registering the order to the Child Support Enforcement Division of the Department of Social Services. Once an out-of-state order is registered in the Registry of Foreign Support, it has the same effect and is subject to the same procedures and defenses as an order of a South Carolina court and it may be enforced and satisfied in the same manner.

CHAPTER FIVE

Issues That Sometimes Arise After Divorce

Enforcing or Modifying Agreements

The ability to enforce an agreement may depend on whether it is in writing, whether it violates laws or public policies, and whether it involves children. The Family Court has exclusive jurisdiction over issues relating to children. Therefore, it has the authority to rule on the validity and fairness of agreements regarding child support, child custody, or visitation, but the Court is never bound by the terms of such agreements.

If the agreement in question was incorporated into a court order, see the following section on enforcing court orders.

If the agreement was not incorporated into a court order, the only recourse when a dispute arises may be to file a lawsuit against the offending party and ask a judge either to enforce the agreement or to award damages resulting from the breach. Depending on the nature of the agreement and the status of the marital relationship, the appropriate court to decide the dispute may be the Family Court, the Circuit Court of Common Pleas, or Magistrate's Court.

As a general rule, an agreement can be modified only with the consent of all parties who entered into it.

If you have a concern about an agreement, you may find it worthwhile to consult with a lawyer about its enforceability, preferably before signing it.

Enforcing Family Court Orders

Contempt of Court

The most common way to enforce an order of the Family Court is to ask the Court to hold someone in contempt of court for failing to comply with the order. All courts, including Family Courts, have the power to enforce their orders by finding violators in contempt of court. If a person is found to have willfully violated, neglected, or refused to obey or perform any order, the judge can rule that the person is in contempt of court and put the person in jail or impose a fine, or both.

There are two kinds of contempt: civil and criminal. Civil contempt is the form most often pursued in the Family Court. The primary purpose of civil contempt is to exact compliance with the Court's orders, not to punish the violator. Therefore, a person who is sent to jail for civil contempt will be released upon doing whatever is required to comply with the order.

The Court must find that the contempt was willful. It should not send anyone to jail for contempt if the person was truly unable to comply with the order.

Voluntary payments of cash or gifts that do not conform to the terms of a support order will not be credited against arrearages and will not serve as a defense to a contempt action. Child support payments must be paid in the manner required by the Court.

Money Judgments and Property Divisions

Orders that require one spouse to pay the other spouse a sum of money or to transfer ownership of property can be enforced by filing a motion to hold the defaulting party in contempt of court. In addition, a lien can be filed against the assets of the debtor that will prevent the debtor from mortgaging or selling any recorded property until the debt is paid. Or a lawsuit to collect the debt can be filed in Magistrate's or Circuit Court (depending on the value of the debt).

Child Visitation

Parents can enforce some provisions of a visitation order without the assistance of a lawyer. Family Court Rule 27 provides a process for either parent to ask the Family Court, by *pro se* affidavit, for a hearing to determine whether the other parent is in contempt of court for violating certain provisions of a visitation order.

The Clerk of the Family Court is required to issue a rule to show cause whenever a person requests relief pursuant to Rule 27. The Rule also provides that a hearing must be held within 30 days of the date on which the *pro se* affidavit is filed. Service of process is the responsibilty of the person requesting the relief.

Child Support

Ordinarily, proceedings for contempt of court are initiated with a motion filed by the complaining party, that is, the person who is supposed to receive the money. A custodial parent can initiate a contempt action for nonpayment of court-ordered health, medical, educational, or other expenses (excluding child support payments) by using an authorized affidavit and supporting documents. More information can be obtained from a Family Court Clerk's office.

If a person falls behind on child support payments that are being made through the Family Court , the Clerk of the Family Court automatically issues a rule to show cause and an affidavit identifying the order of the Court that requires such payment to be made and the amount of arrears and directing the party in arrears to appear in court at a specific time and date. The Clerk of Court is also required to give notice of a show cause hearing to the person who is receiving the support. A person who is owed support is not required to attend the hearing. The hearing will proceed whether or not the person owed support is present. If you receive such a notice, you may want to seek advice from the lawyer who helped obtain the support order about whether you should attend the hearing and what you should do at the hearing if you decide to attend.

In addition to contempt of court, there are many other ways to enforce child support obligations.

Society in general and the federal government in particular have become much less tolerant of people who fail to support their children adequately. Nonsupporting parents face a growing list of negative consequences. For example, nonsupport of children is a basis for terminating parental rights. Also, a parent who does not provide support for a child may be denied workers' compensation death benefits upon the death of the child, and a nonsupporting parent may be denied the right to inherit from a child who dies without leaving a will. A parent who does not provide support for a child may be denied a share of damages awarded by a jury in a wrongful death action arising from the death of a child.

The most effective way to enforce a support obligation of someone who has a regular job is to garnish his or her wages, that is, to have the employer take it out of the person's check and send it directly to the Family Court. Income is subject to immediate withholding when a child support order is issued or modified, without waiting for a missed payment. Income withholding legislation grants the Family Court authority to direct a person's employer (or other payer) to withhold from the person's monthly pay an amount equal to one month's regularly scheduled support payment, plus costs, and plus an additional amount toward any support that is already overdue. Income withholding may also be ordered to pay health insurance premiums.

Many Family Court judges will give a supporting parent a chance to make payments directly to the custodial parent and thereby avoid paying the Family Court's 5% service fee. If the parent fails to make a payment on time, however, the child support order will frequently allow the custodial parent to force future payments to be paid through the Family Court simply by filing an affidavit stating that a child support payment was late.

When a child support arrearage occurs, a lien may be recorded against the obligor's property. Upon recording, the arrearage has the same force and effect as a judgment and it is cumulative to the extent of any and all past due support, until the arrearage is paid in full.

The Family Court has the authority to require a supporting spouse to maintain life insurance or to provide other security to guarantee the payment of child support but only if there are compelling reasons to do so. Presumably, compelling reasons would include a history of reluctance to comply with court orders, an unstable financial history, or other indications of a potential problem in actually having the money paid on time over a period of time.

Some powerful enforcement tools are available to people who use the services of the Child Support Enforcement Division of the Department of Social Services (the Division) that are not available to clients of private lawyers. This is because federal legislation requires states to provide these weapons to state agencies that provide child support services using federal funds. Anyone is eligible to receive the services of the Division without charge. You do not have to be poor.

Seizure of Property: The Division can demand that a person surrender to the Division any property in that person's possession upon which a lien has been perfected, if the amount of unpaid child support exceeds $1,000 and the obligor has been given 30 days notice of the unpaid obligation. Also, financial institutions are required, upon request by the Division, to freeze or surrender deposits, credits, or other personal property they hold on behalf of people who are subject to child support liens.

License Revocation: Once a person falls more than 60 days behind on child support payments, the Division must request licensing authorities to revoke any certificates or licenses held by the obligor, unless the defendant within 90 days of receiving notice has paid the arrearages owed or has signed a consent agreement with the Division establishing a schedule for payment of the arrearage. Revocation is accomplished simply by giving notice to the licensing entity that the license should be revoked. "License" is defined very broadly to include any "authorization issued by a licensing entity that allows an individual or is required of an individual to engage in a business, occupation, or profession." This includes business licenses, teaching certificates, driving licenses, hunting licenses, and professional licenses, including medical licenses (licenses to practice law are excluded, since the South Carolina Supreme Court regulates the practice of law).

Upon revocation, a defendant may appeal the revocation but can contest only two issues: whether he is the obligor and whether he is in compliance with the support order. The license will only be reissued when either the arrearage has been paid in full or a plan has been established with the Division for payment of the arrearage.

Denial or revocation of passport: Federal law allows the denial or revocation of passports of people who owe more than $5,000 in past due child support.

Federal and state income tax refunds: The Division can require that tax refunds be withheld for past due child support. Tax refunds can be intercepted even if the parent is making periodic payments toward the arrearage pursuant to a court order or even if the delinquent amount has been placed in abeyance by court order.

Full collection by Internal Revenue Service: The Division may request assistance from the Internal Revenue Service (IRS) to enforce support obligations. The effect of the process is the creation of a tax lien and treatment of the support judgment as an equivalent to back taxes owed to the federal government.

Unemployment insurance benefits interception: The Division is authorized to intercept unemployment insurance benefits if the recipient is behind on child support payments.

Employer new hire reporting program: All employers are required to report to the Division each month any newly hired and rehired employees. This information is put into a national database to help locate parents who are not paying child support.

Consumer credit reporting: The Division provides consumer credit reporting agencies a monthly report of parents who are two months behind in their child support payments. This only applies to those support orders that are being enforced by the Division.

Nonsupport of a spouse or a child is a criminal offense under South Carolina and federal law. State prosecutions are rare because the Family Court's contempt powers can also produce a jail term, and it is easier to have someone held in contempt by the Family Court than it is to have them convicted of criminal nonsupport. However, the Solicitor in each circuit has the discretion to bring criminal charges.

A more serious threat of prosecution for not paying child support exists under federal law. The Child Support Recovery Act of 1992 makes it a federal crime for a person to fail to pay a past due support obligation created by a court order to a child who resides in another state, if the support has remained unpaid for a period longer than one year or if the amount owed is greater than $5,000. The penalty for a first offense is a fine or six months, or both; for a second or subsequent offense, the penalty is a fine or two years, or both. The Court is also required to order restitution equal to the amount of child support owed at the time of sentencing.

Providing money and support to help a deadbeat parent avoid prosecution can result in federal criminal prosecution for harboring a fugitive and accessory after the act, even if the assistance is provided by the deadbeat parent's new spouse.

Modifying Family Court Orders

Only a Family Court judge can modify a Family Court order. Until an order is modified by a Family Court judge, either spouse can elect to enforce the requirements of the order (see the preceding section on enforcing Family Court orders).

Modifying Orders When Both Parties Agree

If you and your spouse or former spouse agree that some provision of a Family Court order should be changed or should not be enforced, one of you should ask a lawyer to help you obtain a modified order from the Family Court. When both parties agree to the change, a modification can usually be accomplished fairly quickly and inexpensively. The Family Court's primary concerns will be whether the agreement to modify the order was made voluntarily and without duress and whether the modified terms would be fair (fairness is particularly important when the change would affect children).

Even if you and your spouse agree that some provision of the order should be modified or not complied with, you should continue to comply with the order until it is modified by a Family Court judge. Unless the order is modified by a Family Court judge, either of you can change your mind and insist that the terms of the order be strictly enforced and, perhaps, even have the noncomplying spouse held in contempt of court.

If both parties decide to disregard some aspects of a Family Court order without obtaining a modification, the potential consequences for doing so will depend on the nature of the terms that are violated and whether or not documentation exists to prove that both parties voluntarily agreed to the change. For example, former spouses are encouraged to be flexible about child visitation schedules. Therefore, a Family Court judge is not likely to be concerned about voluntary variations from a court-ordered visitation schedule (but remember that either party can insist on returning to strict compliance with the court-ordered schedule until the order is modified by a judge). On the other hand, an agreement to pay less child support than was ordered by the Family Court is never binding on the children unless it is approved by the Family Court. Thus, even if both parents agree to reduce the amount of child support, the custodial parent may change his or her mind, then seek to enforce the terms of the order. It is also possible that the children themselves may be entitled to recover the difference between what was paid and what was ordered, plus interest, even after they become adults.

If you want to do something other than what a Family Court order requires, you should consult a lawyer before doing it, even if your spouse (or former spouse) agrees. If you decide not to consult a lawyer, you should at least clearly describe the terms of your agreement in a written document signed and dated by both parties (and preferably notarized). Without clear evidence that the change was agreed to by both parties, the person who is obligated under the order to pay, to do, or to refrain from doing something will be at risk of being held in contempt of court for violating the order, if the other party has a change of heart later (it happens). For example, if the agreement is to pay less alimony than required by the order and the judge is not persuaded that the supported spouse consented to the reduction, was unfairly pressured to do so, or the reduction was unfair, the Family Court has the power, not only to put the supporting spouse in jail for not paying the full amount, but also to require full payment of the amount that should have been paid under the order, perhaps plus interest. While a written agreement between the parties is not binding on the Family Court and will not provide complete protection from court-ordered sanctions, it may protect you from being held in willful contempt of the Family Court and possibly sentenced to jail.

Property Division

The general rule is that property divisions are not modifiable by the Family Court unless one of the parties engaged in fraud or there is some other compelling reason to reexamine the fairness of the property division. If both parties agree to a change, however, a Family Court judge may be willing to modify the order.

Alimony

If alimony was not requested or awarded at the time of divorce, the Family Court is not permitted to award it at a later time. If alimony is awarded during the divorce process, some but not all forms of alimony can be modified by the Family Court if there was a significant and unanticipated change in either the needs of the receiving party for alimony or the ability of the other party to pay alimony.

Any person receiving alimony should consult with a lawyer before establishing a long-term relationship with a paramour.

A relationship with a paramour may warrant a termination of alimony, if the relationship is tantamount to marriage. A key to finding a relationship is tantamount to marriage is whether the supported spouse and the paramour are economically relying on one another. Simply proving that a former spouse is in a romantic relationship is not enough to terminate alimony, if the paramours maintain separate residences and do not live together continuously for an extended period of time.

Another way that alimony can be terminated is pursuant to a statute which provides that alimony can be terminated if a supported spouse "resides with another person in a romantic relationship for a period of ninety or more consecutive days. The Court may determine that a continued cohabitation exists if there is evidence that the supported spouse lives with another person for periods of less than ninety days and the two periodically separate in order to circumvent the ninety-day requirement."

If the parties have an agreement that alimony cannot be modified, then it may not matter that the supported spouse is living with a paramour.

Advanced age, alone, does not justify a reduction in alimony. Retirement, however, does warrant a hearing to evaluate whether there has been a substantial change of circumstances.

Child Support

Child support is subject to the continuing review of the Family Court. The Family Court can modify child support awards as circumstances warrant, but usually only upon a showing of an unanticipated significant or material change in a child's needs or the ability of one or both parents to pay support.

If you are paying child support and believe that you should be entitled to a reduction in your payments (because you lost your job, for example), you should file a petition in Family Court as soon as possible. You should not wait for the Child Support Enforcement Division of DSS to work through its caseload and procedures. Actions to increase or decrease child support obligations can be initiated by unrepresented parties by using the free "Self-Represented Litigant Child Support Modification Packets" that are on the judicial department's website. The forms are available at http://www.sccourts.org/forms/indexSRLChildSupport.cfm.

The fact that one of several children has become 18 years old does not affect a parent's child support obligation absent a Family Court order modifying the amount owed.

Extraordinary medical expenses that were not provided for or anticipated at the time of the child support award constitute changed circumstances on which an adjustment of child support can be based.

A need for orthodontic work or other special medical care might justify an increase in child support under some circumstances.

The remarriage of a spouse in and of itself is not a change of conditions sufficient to justify a decrease in the amount of child support. Remarriage of the custodial parent does not ordinarily terminate a person's child support obligations. The reason for this is simple: the new spouse of the custodial parent has no obligation to maintain the new stepchildren.

A child support order issued by another state can be modified by a South Carolina court only if it is registered with the Family Court and, after notice and hearing, the Court finds that:

1. neither the child, the obligee, nor the obligor reside in the issuing state, the nonresident plaintiff seeks modification, and the defendant is subject to the jurisdiction of the Family Court; or

2. a party who is a natural person (not an agency) or the child is subject to the personal jurisdiction of the Family Court and all the parties who are natural persons have filed an agreement in the issuing tribunal providing that the Family Court may modify the support order and assume continuing, exclusive jurisdiction over the order.

Child Custody and Visitation

The Family Court has continuing jurisdiction to reconsider the best interests of a child in the event that circumstances change and the welfare of the child would be served by changing custody. The Family Court must apply the same standard in deciding whether to alter joint or shared custody arrangements as it does in deciding whether to change custody from one parent to the other: whether there has been a material change of circumstances substantially affecting the child's welfare.

The burden of proving the nature and extent of the changed circumstances is on the party who is seeking the change. There are no hard and fast rules, rather the totality of the circumstances will be considered. Remarriage alone is an insufficient basis for changing custody. Custody is not to be changed unless a betterment to the child will result. If a child is happy, content, and thriving in the current environment, it is unlikely that custody will be changed.

Parents with custody should make every effort to foster healthy relationships between their children and noncustodial parents. One mother lost custody of her 14-year-old daughter because the mother pressured the daughter to view the mother and father as adversaries and exhibited a pattern of inflexibility and uncooperativeness in her dealings with the father.

The Family Court can modify the amount and conditions of a noncustodial parent's visitation rights, including termination or suspension, if a showing is made that a change would be in the best interests of a child. The power to terminate visitation is a drastic action that will be exercised sparingly.

Proposed relocations of children's residences usually require visitation and sometimes custody arrangements to be reconsidered. Disputes about relocation present some of the knottiest and most disturbing problems that our courts are called on to resolve. The search for a fair resolution of relocation cases has vexed courts nationwide. This is because a collision of interests occurs when one parent decides to relocate with a child and the other parent objects. The relocating parent's interest is in exercising freedom to move to a more desirable location and the non-relocating parent's interest is in maintaining convenient access to the child. While parents are fighting to advance their own interests, they and the courts sometimes forget to focus on the best interests of the children.

The South Carolina legislature declared in 1996 that a court must have compelling reasons to prevent a parent from relocating with a child to another place within South Carolina. Thus, a custodial parent living in Rock Hill who wants to move with a child to Charleston, over 200 miles away, cannot be prevented from doing so unless compelling reasons exist, yet whether a custodial parent would be allowed to move the same child to Charlotte, North Carolina, less than 20 miles away, will be determined by a best interests of the child analysis. In 2004, the South Carolina Supreme Court abolished the presumption against relocation rule it had established in 1982 and determined that a noncustodial parent who seeks a change of custody due to the actual or proposed relocation of the custodial parent must establish the following: (1) there has been a substantial change in circumstances affecting the welfare of the child and (2) a change in custody is in the best interests of the child.

It should be noted that, even under the prior test, South Carolina courts have generally allowed custodial parents to relocate with the children, even though it significantly affected the relationship between the children and the noncustodial parents. There have been some exceptions, however, and noncustodial parents who are interested in seeking a change of custody because the custodial parent is relocating should consult a lawyer.

Special Custody and Visitation Rules When Military Members are Deployed

The Military Parent Equal Protection Act provides some special rules for custody, visitation, and support when a military parent is required to be separated from a child due to military service.

"Military service" has two meanings. For active duty personnel, it means a deployment that does not permit a family member to accompany the parent on the deployment. For members of the National Guard, it means a call to active service for a period of more than 30 days.

If a military parent is required to be separated from a child due to military service, the Family Court cannot enter a final order modifying the custody or visitation terms in an existing order until 90 days after the military parent is released from military service. Military service alone cannot be the sole reason for permanently modifying custody or visitation.

An existing child custody or visitation order can be temporarily modified to make reasonable accommodation because of the military parent's service. A temporary modification "automatically terminates when the military parent is released from service and, upon release, the original terms of the custody or visitation order in place at the time military parent was called to military service are automatically reinstated." A temporary modification order must provide for custody or reasonable visitation when the military parent has a leave from military service.

If no temporary modification order is issued, the nonmilitary parent must make any children reasonably available to the military parent when the military parent has leave from military service.

If there is no existing custody or visitation order and it appears that military service is imminent, the Family Court is required, upon motion of either parent, to expedite a temporary hearing to establish temporary custody or visitation, establish support, and provide other appropriate relief.

If military necessity precludes court adjudication before mobilization, "the parties are encouraged to negotiate mutually agreeable arrangements prior to mobilization." The parents are *required* to cooperate with each other to resolve custody, visitation, and child support.

If either parent does not reasonably accommodate the other parent, fails to provide income and earnings information in a timely manner, or causes unreasonable delay, the Family Court may consider such conduct in awarding attorneys' fees and costs.

Bankruptcy

Overview

A bankruptcy proceeding that is filed before, during, or after a divorce can have a significant impact on the outcome of the divorce action. If you are contemplating divorce, you should consult with a lawyer if there is any possibility that you or your spouse might file for bankruptcy. Bankruptcy law is a complex field of law with many pitfalls for the unwary. The information in this chapter only provides a bare bones overview of key concepts about bankruptcy.

The purpose of bankruptcy proceedings is to offer debtors opportunities for fresh starts. The Bankruptcy Code gives debtors two ways to deal with debt loads that are too heavy for them to manage: (1) by providing a structure for paying off the debts or part of them without losing ownership of their property (reorganization), or (2) by employing a procedure through which they are discharged from responsibility for their debts by selling the debtors' assets, even if this does not produce enough cash to fully pay off the debts (liquidation). The Bankruptcy Code is divided into chapters, with Chapters 11, 12, and 13, being concerned with rehabilitation, and Chapter 7 with liquidation.

Some debts and other obligations will not be relieved in a bankruptcy proceeding, that is, the debtor will continue to have responsibility for them. Bankruptcy laws favor enforcement of familial support obligations over a "fresh start" of the debtor. Bankruptcy proceedings under Chapters 7, 11, 12, or 13 do not release debtors from alimony or support obligations owed to a spouse, former spouse, or child if the obligation arose from a separation agreement, judgment of divorce, or property settlement and the debt has not been assigned to a third party other than the government. The spouse, former spouse, or child has priority over some other unsecured creditors. Until 1994, debts created by property divisions between spouses were dischargeable in bankruptcy. Today, it is possible in many circumstances to prevent debts from being discharged if they arose pursuant to the division of marital property.

Chapter 7 bankruptcies involve the liquidation of the debtors' assets. An individual, a husband and wife together, a business, or a partnership may elect to file for liquidation under Chapter 7. As with all chapters, debtors report all assets and liabilities and claim exemptions pursuant to state laws that protect certain property from creditors. A Chapter 7 trustee is appointed to determine whether there is equity in the debtor's property that is available for distribution to creditors. If there is, the case is deemed an "asset case" and the trustee liquidates the estate.

Any assets produced by liquidating the estate are first applied to administrative expenses. Secured creditors have priority over unsecured creditors up to the value of the assets that serve as collateral for their claims. Priority creditors are paid next. This includes debts such as tax claims, unpaid wages, and most alimony and other support obligations. Unsecured creditors share any remaining assets on a *pro rata* basis.

Most cases filed under Chapter 7 are "no asset" cases due to liens that encumber the debtor's property and due to the debtor's exemptions. Creditors will not receive a distribution from the bankruptcy court in a "no asset" case, and the debtor will retain all property, subject to the claims of secured creditors.

Chapter 13 bankruptcies are known as "wage earner" plans, and they may be filed by an individual, or a husband and wife together, provided the debtor has a regular source of income. Businesses cannot file Chapter 13 bankruptcies. The debtor proposes a plan to repay creditors over a three to five year period by making payments to a Chapter 13 trustee, who in turn distributes the money to creditors. Only the debtor may propose a plan in a Chapter 13, not the creditors. There are limits on how much a person can owe and still seek Chapter 13 protection. Unsecured debts must total less than $250,000, and secured debts must total less than $750,000.

Property of the Bankruptcy Estate

The property of the bankruptcy estate is all property in which the debtor has a legal or equitable interest when the bankruptcy petition is filed. This includes proceeds, products, offerings, rents, or profits from such property. Property acquired within 180 days of the filing of the petition by bequest, devise, or inheritance, as a result of a marital property settlement agreement or divorce decree, or as a beneficiary of a life insurance policy or death benefit plan, will also become property of the estate.

The bankruptcy trustee may be able to demand the return of the debtor's property from a third party. For example, a trustee may be able to set aside preferential transfers or fraudulent conveyances, or to demand the turnover of property from a creditor that repossessed property prior to bankruptcy. These rights would not be available to a debtor outside of bankruptcy, but they are granted to the trustee by the Bankruptcy Code.

There are limits to the extent that transfers between spouses can be set aside. For example, a trustee may not set aside a transfer if the transfer is a good faith alimony or support payment to a spouse, former spouse, or child of the debtor, and if it was made pursuant to a valid separation agreement, divorce decree, or other order of a court of record, and it has not been assigned.

Some assets may be kept out of a bankruptcy proceeding. These are called exempted assets. Exemptions allow debtors to prevent some property from being used to satisfy their debts. A few examples of exempted property in South Carolina include: homestead, $5,000; motor vehicle, $1,200; household furnishings and goods, clothing, appliances, books, animals, crops, musical instruments, $2,500; jewelry, $500; professionally prescribed health aids, no limit; tools of the trade, $750; and state employee retirement system benefits, no limit.

Exceptions to Discharge

Alimony and child support are generally not dischargeable. A bankruptcy discharge does not affect the debtor's obligation to pay spousal and child support. An order for payment of support must satisfy a two-prong test before the debt will be declared not dischargeable by the bankruptcy court: first, the obligation must be payable on behalf of a spouse, former spouse, or child; and, second, the obligation must be in the nature of alimony, maintenance, or support.

A debt for alimony, maintenance, or support that is not dischargeable under bankruptcy law becomes dischargeable if it is assigned to another entity voluntarily, by operation of law, or otherwise, except child support that is assigned to a state in exchange for child support. Thus, for example, some courts have held that if a spouse who wins an award of past due child support assigns this right to her attorney, the debt becomes dischargeable in bankruptcy.

Debts arising from property divisions between divorcing spouses are not dischargeable unless the debtor spouse cannot otherwise support himself or his dependents or continue operating his business, or unless the detriment to him of paying the debt outweighs the detriment to the spouse of nonpayment. The factors to be examined in determining whether the benefits of discharging the debtor's property-related divorce debts outweigh the detrimental consequences to the nondebtor spouse include, but are not limited to: the incomes and expenses of both parties; whether the nondebtor spouse is jointly liable on the debts; the number of dependents; the nature of the debts; reaffirmation of any debts; and the nondebtor spouse's ability to pay.

Automatic Stay

An automatic stay is imposed when a bankruptcy action is filed. This prohibits any disposition of or collection attempts against property of the bankrupt person's estate. The stay takes effect immediately upon the filing of a bankruptcy petition without notice. This can impede marital litigation unless relief from the stay is granted by the bankruptcy court.

The automatic stay does not prevent the commencement or continuation of an action or proceeding to establish paternity; establish or modify alimony, maintenance, or support; or collect alimony, maintenance, and support from property that is not part of the bankrupt estate. However, it may be prudent to seek relief from the stay before proceeding in such actions.

Remarriage

Remarriage to Each Other

Some people remarry each other after going through a divorce. Once the divorce is over, divorced people are free to marry whomever they choose, even each other. The legal considerations involved with marrying a person a second time are really no different than those that apply when people marry for the first time.

If the divorce produced a court order or an agreement requiring certain things to be done, the unfulfilled requirements of the order or agreement are mooted by the remarriage, but those transactions that have been completed would not be affected. For example, if an agreement settling the divorce calls for the husband to transfer the title to the marital home to his wife, the agreement would be negated if the title to the house had not been changed by the time of the remarriage. If the title was changed before the remarriage, the house would be the nonmarital property of the wife and any cash she paid her husband for his interest in the house would be the nonmarital property of the husband. They could agree to retransfer everything upon remarriage, but they would not have to do so.

Child custody and visitation would not be issues following remarriage, and there would no longer be a reason to continue paying child support or spousal support. A general principle of law, however, is that a court order that requires someone to do something or to refrain from doing something will remain in effect until a judge decides to change it. In the interest of caution, therefore, people who remarry each other should consult with a lawyer to determine whether they need to have the Family Court formally terminate any portions of the divorce decree with which they no longer need to comply. This is especially important when child support payments are being paid through the Family Court.

Remarriage to Someone Else

It is very common for divorced people to marry new husbands or wives. Such remarriages do not have any automatic legal consequences that affect the terms of the divorce, except that the person who remarries will no longer be entitled to receive spousal support, unless an agreement or court order says otherwise.

Depending on any number of factors, a remarriage might create a sufficient change in circumstances to affect child custody and visitation or the amount of child or spousal support that should be paid. Any divorced person who is thinking about marrying again or who has already remarried should consult with a lawyer to find out whether the marriage might affect the terms of the divorce.

CHAPTER SIX

Hiring and Working with a Lawyer

Determining If You Need a Lawyer

Most people need a lawyer to help them through the divorce process. Dismantling a marriage is a complicated process filled with risks of personal conflict and financial disaster. Even the simplest, most amicable divorce requires both parties to make very important decisions under highly emotional circumstances. There are few people who have the time, the nerves, and the know how to represent themselves in divorces. Even divorce lawyers hire lawyers to help them get through the termination of their marriages.

If you are determined to represent yourself in Family Court, you are allowed to do so, but it will not be easy. You cannot count on the Family Court judge overlooking any irregularities in your documents or evidence.

Instructions and forms for processing simple divorces have been approved by the South Carolina Supreme Court. "Self-represented litigant divorce packets" are available for free at http://www.sccourts.org/forms/indexSRLdivorcepacket.cfm. The forms are intended for use by people: (1) who have no marital property or marital debts or have reached an agreement on how to divide their property and debts; and (2) who have no children and expect none or have minor children and have reached an agreement as to custody and visitation as well as an amount of child support that meets the minimum requirements set by the South Carolina Child Support Guidelines.

It may be particularly tempting not to hire a lawyer if you are the defendant. After all, even if you do nothing your spouse will prosecute the divorce and you will be just as divorced as your spouse is when it is over. If you have no children, no cash or other property to be divided, nor any other issues to resolve other than the divorce, and if the divorce is being sought on the no fault ground after a year of separation, there may be no need for you to hire a lawyer.

If your spouse serves pleadings on you that include notice of a temporary (*pendente lite*) hearing, you should seek legal advice without delay. Temporary hearings can be very important events in marital litigation (see additional discussion in Chapter Three), and a lawyer will need as much time as possible to prepare.

If the divorce is at all complicated, or if you are the one who wants to bring the divorce action, it is almost a necessity to hire a lawyer to navigate the various stages of a divorce proceeding. How much help you need from a lawyer will depend on the length of the marriage, the amount of property to be divided, whether there are any minor children, the level of hostility between you and your spouse, and many other factors. Most lawyers will charge you a relatively small fee to help you evaluate whether you need a lawyer and to predict how much it would cost to handle your divorce or to provide whatever service you are seeking. Some lawyers will provide such an analysis free of charge.

You should consider hiring a lawyer to make sure that you understand the legal issues and your rights in the divorce. Most lawyers will advise you about these matters without insisting on handling the entire divorce.

A lawyer cannot represent both parties in a divorce action, even if both spouses want to hire one lawyer. It is not uncommon for two people who are thinking about divorce to consider hiring one lawyer to handle the divorce or to draft a separation agreement. This is especially true when the parties are getting along well and do not intend to fight over anything. Hiring one lawyer would save money and make it less likely that disputes would arise during the divorce process. A lawyer cannot agree to represent both spouses, however. In fact, lawyers in South Carolina are prohibited from representing both spouses in a divorce or even from advising a couple about their legal rights. This is because the divorce process is at heart an adversarial process and a lawyer would have impossibly divided loyalties trying to represent the interests of both the husband and wife. For example, if the parties presented the lawyer with a proposed property settlement agreement, the lawyer could not advise one spouse that the agreement seemed to unfairly favor the other spouse without violating his duty of loyalty to the spouse favored by the agreement.

You and your spouse could go together to ask a lawyer to explain the divorce process and to give you information, not advice, about the law. It would be improper, however, for a lawyer to tell both spouses how the law would be applied in their particular case if they decided to seek a divorce. This would be legal advice, and a lawyer cannot give legal advice to two people who have differing interests. Owing to the fine line between information and advice, most divorce lawyers in South Carolina are unwilling to meet with both the husband and the wife for any purpose.

By way of illustration, assume that a married couple wants to know how their property would be divided if they file for divorce. Before a lawyer could answer this, he would need to ask questions about the many factors that a judge would consider before dividing the property. These factors include such things as who acquired the property (including who earned the money that went toward its purchase and who made indirect contributions such as housecleaning and yard work), what each spouse thought each item of property was worth, who did the most during the marriage to maintain the property or otherwise affect its value, which items of property were the most important to each spouse, and even who was at fault in the breakdown of the marriage (for a more complete discussion of the factors, see the discussion of property division in Chapter Four). It is very likely that both spouses would want some of the information about these factors kept secret from the other spouse. If so, this would put the lawyer in a hopelessly difficult position and make it impossible for the lawyer to give candid, professional advice to both spouses.

Even if both parties say they want their property to be divided fairly, people frequently disagree about what is fair (or even what is fifty-fifty), and it is basic human nature for each person to want to get as much of the property as possible when it is being divided in a divorce. Divorce is an adversarial process and divorce lawyers must be free to be advocates for their clients'– and only their clients'– positions.

Discussing the Case with Your Spouse's Lawyer

When should you discuss the case with your spouse's lawyer? The short answer is almost never. The preceding section explains some of the reasons why one lawyer is not allowed to represent both spouses in a divorce. Divorce is an adversarial process, and divorce lawyers are professionally obliged to represent the interests of only one party in a divorce proceeding. Thus, your spouse's lawyer's job is to represent the best interests of your spouse, not you, and to pursue your spouse's goals in the divorce, not yours. Nothing that you say to your spouse's attorney is protected by the attorney-client privilege, and like criminal confessions, you can expect that anything you say to your spouse's lawyer can and will be used against you if it will benefit your spouse's interests in the divorce.

If you have your own lawyer, it is highly improper for your spouse's lawyer to contact you directly about anything, unless you and your lawyer approve it. If you are ever contacted by your spouse's lawyer (or anyone working for that lawyer) after you have hired a lawyer, tell the person that you are represented by counsel, provide your lawyer's name and number, refuse to talk to your spouse's lawyer, and notify your lawyer at once. By the same token, if you are represented by a lawyer, you should not contact your spouse's lawyer directly. That is your lawyer's job. If you become frustrated that your lawyer is not moving fast enough, the solution is to try to resolve your complaint with your lawyer, not to try to take matters into your own hands.

If you do not have a lawyer, it is not only proper but also necessary for your spouse's lawyer to contact you and for you to contact the lawyer. For one thing, you will need to exchange relevant information about the divorce. (Even if you decide not to hire a lawyer to handle the divorce for you, you may want to hire a lawyer to advise you about what kinds of information you should seek from your spouse and to advise you about the limits of what your spouse can require you to disclose.) Although formal discovery techniques can be used if permission is obtained from the Family Court, the Family Court Rules encourage both sides to a divorce to exchange information voluntarily in order to save time and money. You are required to exchange forms providing financial information (Financial Declaration forms are available from the Clerk of the Family Court).

If you have a face-to-face meeting with your spouse's lawyer, it would be a good idea to make a recording of the conversation in case any disagreements arise later about what was said.

It is appropriate for an attorney who represents one spouse to discuss possible settlement terms with the other spouse, if the other spouse is not represented by a lawyer. Unfortunately, some lawyers step over the line and give legal advice to opposing parties, perhaps inadvertently. In settlement negotiations with an unrepresented party, a lawyer is allowed to explain what her client wants and to explain why proposed settlement offers are acceptable or unacceptable to her client. An attorney is not allowed to give an unrepresented spouse any legal or personal advice other than to hire his or her own lawyer. An attorney is not supposed to offer opinions about the probable outcome of a trial to an unrepresented spouse or to explain how the law either supports her client's position or does not support the position of the unrepresented spouse. This would be legal advice, which a lawyer is not allowed to give to an unrepresented opposing party. As a result, many lawyers will only communicate with unrepresented parties in writing to avoid any appearance that they are exerting improper influence and to have a clear record of all communications.

If your spouse's lawyer tries to tell you about your legal rights or how a judge will decide the outcome of your case, this is unprofessional conduct that should be reported to the South Carolina Supreme Court's Commission on Lawyer Conduct by writing to The Commission on Lawyer Conduct, 1220 Senate Street, Suite 305, Columbia, South Carolina 29201. Include as much detail as possible about what happened and enclose copies of any documents or recordings that might support your complaint. Be sure to include your name and address as well as that of the lawyer. You cannot report lawyer misconduct online or over the telephone.

Hiring a Lawyer

Locating a Competent, Affordable Lawyer

You should be comfortable with your lawyer. You should have confidence in your lawyer's ability to handle your case. You should trust your lawyer to be honest with you. You should even like your lawyer. There is no reason to go through a divorce feeling bad about your lawyer. Lawyers come in many different sizes, styles, and personalities. They also come in many different price ranges. You should be able to find one who fits your needs. This is really not hard to accomplish, and any time you spend selecting the right lawyer for you will be rewarded many times over.

It is really important to find a lawyer whose philosophy of law practice is compatible with your goals and values. All lawyers will try to achieve their clients' goals in a divorce, but some lawyers perceive goals in terms of positive results on contested issues while other lawyers take a much broader perspective and consider the overall goals and values of their clients rather than just the issues at dispute in the divorce. One competent lawyer may be aggressive and hard-hitting while another competent lawyer may place an emphasis on trying to preserve friendly relationships among all participants to the divorce. One lawyer may pursue every possible way to gain an advantage over the other side, while another lawyer may only do what is reasonably necessary to help the client get through the divorce without being taken advantage of by the other spouse. Some lawyers encourage their clients to seek alternative methods to resolve their disputes, such as mediation, but others prefer negotiation and litigation.

A lawyer's philosophy of lawyering is something that a divorce lawyer should discuss at the initial meeting with you, or you should ask about it. If your vision of what a lawyer should do for you and how it should be done is not the same as your lawyer's vision of family law practice, you will not be happy with your lawyer.

When you start looking for a lawyer, don't plan to hire the first one you meet, although you may decide to do so if you feel completely comfortable with the first lawyer. You should plan to interview at least two lawyers; more if the first two don't feel right. Remember that you are buying a service, and lawyers are selling a service. You have the money; they have the product. Law practice is a business as well as a profession. If a lawyer wants your business, the lawyer should treat you like a valued customer, especially at the beginning of the relationship. Don't be embarrassed to do some comparison shopping.

The best way to find a lawyer is often to ask friends and relatives for recommendations. People who have been through divorces and who would recommend their lawyers to you can also tell you how those lawyers interacted with them and describe their philosophies of law practice. Sometimes, your friends might even recommend hiring the lawyers who represented their spouses. Be sure to ask anyone who recommends a lawyer to tell you what they liked and disliked about the lawyer. Attributes that appealed to them may not suit you.

If you have had any prior experiences with lawyers, for example in real estate closings, you could ask those lawyers to recommend some divorce lawyers to you. They either know or can easily find out about the reputations of divorce lawyers in your community. Similarly, friends and relatives who have used lawyers for reasons other than divorces can ask their former lawyers to recommend divorce lawyers for you.

If you must begin your search without any personal recommendations, you can call the South Carolina Bar's Lawyer Referral Service at 1-800-868-2284 (803-799-7100 in Richland or Lexington County). After you explain where you live and what type of legal problem you have, the referral service will give you the name and number of the next lawyer on the list, but the lawyer must have at least three years of experience in family law. You then call the lawyer yourself.

Lawyers participating in the lawyer referral service can only charge $50 for the first 30 minutes of consultation. Any additional fee beyond that must be negotiated with the lawyer. The Lawyer Referral Service can also be accessed online in the South Carolina Bar website's Public Information section at www.scbar.org.

If you cannot afford to hire a lawyer, you may be eligible for assistance from a South Carolina Legal Services Office. To find out if you qualify, you can call the Legal Aid Telephone Intake Service (LATIS) at 1-888-346-5592. Or you might be able to find a lawyer who will help you for free. Go to www.scbar.org and look for "pro bono resources" in the Public Information section of the website.

The South Carolina Bar website's section on "Public Information" also provides links to pro bono resources (how to get a lawyer if you cannot afford to hire one), Ask-a-Lawyer (where volunteer lawyers answer legal questions for free during certain times on certain days of the week), free clinic information, LawLine (online answers to frequently asked questions), and free publication information.

Another option is to go to the public library or to use the Internet to consult national directories of lawyers that rate some divorce lawyers. Membership in the American Academy of Matrimonial Lawyers (AAML) is by invitation only and serves as evidence that a lawyer is considered a competent divorce lawyer by others in the field.

The Academy's website is at http://www.AAML.org. AAML lawyers tend to charge at the high end of the scale, but this is not universally true, so do not assume that a lawyer will charge more just because he or she is a member of the AAML. Shop around.

Before you make an appointment to see a lawyer, you should try to find out how much the lawyer will charge you (for more information about attorneys' fees, read the following section on "paying attorneys' fees"). Getting this information in advance may avoid wasting your time (and the lawyer's time) talking to a lawyer who charges more than you are willing to pay. Simply call the lawyer's office, explain that you are looking for a lawyer, and ask how much the lawyer charges (including how much the lawyer charges for the initial meeting).

You should also ask the lawyer's office to send you a copy of the lawyer's standard retainer agreement (the contract between the lawyer and the client). Some lawyers are reluctant to give out copies of their retainer agreements. If you cannot get a copy of the agreement in advance, be sure that you take it home after the initial appointment and review it carefully before deciding whether to sign it.

When you call, you may also want to ask how many years the lawyer has practiced law and what percentage of his or her practice is devoted to divorce work. If the office hesitates to provide this information, call someone else. Also consider how you were treated by whomever you talked with on the phone. Were they polite and professional? If not, consider calling a different attorney. During your divorce, you will be making a number of calls to your lawyer's office. You deserve to be treated politely and professionally every time you call.

Meeting With a Lawyer for the First Time

The first meeting with a lawyer is when you begin deciding if you want to hire the lawyer and when the lawyer is deciding whether to accept you as a client. Just as you do not want to hire a bad lawyer, the lawyer does not want to get stuck with a bad client. (We will talk some more about bad clients a little later.)

You should tell the lawyer up front if you have talked to or plan to talk to other lawyers before making a decision. Unless you have an emergency situation, take a day or so to sleep on it and to finish your comparison shopping. Think about what each lawyer said and how you felt about the lawyers, their staffs, and their offices. As a divorce client, you will have a long and somewhat personal relationship with your lawyer. Don't rush into it. If you are not happy with the first lawyers you interview, find another to interview. Once you decide which lawyer to hire, you should as a matter of courtesy inform any other lawyers you considered that you decided not to hire them.

Everything you say to your lawyer is a privileged communication, even conversations that take place before you decide to hire the lawyer. The existence of a privilege means that the lawyer cannot be forced to testify or otherwise reveal your confidential information. Lawyers also have an ethical responsibility to maintain the secrets and confidences of their clients or risk losing their licenses to practice law. What all this means is that you can trust your lawyer to keep your secrets no matter what you say to the lawyer, even if you confess to a crime. The purpose of these rules is to encourage clients to be honest and open with their lawyers so that lawyers can more fully understand their clients' problems and provide professional advice and services.

Only private conversations between clients and attorneys are protected. Therefore, if you talk to your lawyer in the presence of anyone other than members of the lawyer's staff, the conversation may not be considered a protected conversation. Therefore, you should be careful what you say if other people, including friends and relatives, are participating in a conversation with you and your attorney. If you want to have a relative or friend with you during your initial meeting with a lawyer, you should ask the lawyer or someone in the office if this would be acceptable.

At the first meeting, ask the lawyer all the questions you can think of that might make a difference in your hiring decision. You might begin by asking about the length of the lawyer's experience in law practice and with divorce cases. Although it may be a little uncomfortable to do so, you should ask if the lawyer has ever been disciplined by a court for ethical misconduct or successfully sued by a client for malpractice. If so, you should expect a detailed explanation, perhaps including copies of the court orders that detail the findings of misconduct or malpractice. This is a touchy subject to bring up and you want to be tactful. Some lawyers may be afraid that you are the type of client who may be prone to file grievances and decline to represent you. Perhaps it would reduce this risk to show the lawyer that the recommendation to ask about the lawyer's grievance history came out of this book.

If your case will involve a lot of assets or highly disputed issues, you should anticipate the possibility that all issues will not be settled before trial and that the result of a trial might be appealed. If so, it would also be useful to ask how many contested trials the lawyer has handled during the past year. Most divorce cases are settled, but some are not. If the lawyer is not trying any contested cases, it may show a lack of willingness to take cases to trial that should be tried. Conversely, a divorce lawyer who has a high percentage of cases going to trial (more than 25%), may not be settling some cases that should be settled.

Another issue you may want to discuss with the lawyer is how the lawyers uses technology to practice more efficiently. Most divorce lawyers have standard letters and forms that fit almost any aspect of a divorce case. Some have very sophisticated computer systems and other technology that help them work more efficiently. If the lawyer that you are interviewing is technologically astute, the lawyer will be delighted to explain how that technological sophistication translates into better legal services at less cost to you. A lawyer who hesitates or is unable to explain this to you may not be able to handle your case as efficiently as someone else, but this does not necessarily mean that you should not hire that lawyer. The most important factor is whether you trust the lawyer and feel comfortable allowing the lawyer to handle your case.

Don't be shy about asking for an explanation of the fees you will be charged and any other expenses you will be asked to pay (for more information, see the following section on "paying attorneys' fees").

The bottom line is that you should ask a lot of questions before deciding which divorce lawyer to hire. Once you have as much information as you plan to get, you should trust your instincts and hire the lawyer with whom you feel the most comfortable and in whom you have the most confidence.

During the first meeting, the lawyer will probably want you to review the facts of your marital difficulties and outline your objectives. At some point all lawyers will ask divorce clients to provide fairly exhaustive information about themselves, their spouses, their finances, and their marital histories. Some divorce lawyers ask their clients to write detailed descriptions of their marriages, perhaps even before the first meeting. If you do not want to go into that much detail until you've decided which lawyer to hire, explain this to the lawyer. It might save both of you time and money.

You can expect the lawyer to be direct and clear in communicating information to you at the first meeting, and you can expect the lawyer to promise to answer all of your questions within a reasonable period of time. However, you should not expect the lawyer to answer all of your questions at the first meeting. Even the most experienced lawyer cannot instantly recall and explain every nuance of the law that might be relevant to your situation. Also, a divorce lawyer will often need to gather and analyze more information than is available at the first meeting. In divorce cases, it is sometimes impossible to provide some answers or to make accurate predictions about probable results until the other spouse responds to discovery requests, and sometimes not even then.

Entering A Retainer Agreement

"Retainer" is a word that applies to both the contractual agreement between an attorney and a client and the preliminary fee given to the lawyer to secure his or her services or for the work the lawyer does.

Almost all lawyers have written retainer agreements. Some lawyers use retainer agreements that look like formal contracts, while others use a letter format to describe the terms of the attorney-client relationship. Both are appropriate. You should expect the lawyer to provide a written agreement that is clear and easy to understand. If you cannot understand the terms of the retainer agreement, or none is offered, consider hiring someone else.[6]

The topics that are typically covered in a retainer agreement include the services to be performed, any services not to be performed, the fees to be paid and the payment schedule, any additional costs to be borne by the client, and how the contract can be terminated. A common example of a service not to be performed is representing you on appeal. There is no reason for you or the lawyer to become obligated at the beginning of your relationship to continue working together if an appeal is needed. A separate agreement can be created later if the need for representation on appeal arises, or it may turn out that either you or the lawyer decide that it would be better for you to hire someone else to handle the appeal.

It is rarely advisable to sign a retainer agreement or to pay a retainer fee at the first meeting with a lawyer (if the lawyer charges you for the first meeting, you should pay for that, of course, because it is for services that the lawyer has already performed). You need to read over the retainer agreement very carefully. The retainer agreement is a legal document that establishes what you and the lawyer are agreeing to do and what you are agreeing to pay for the lawyer's services. If there is anything in the agreement you do not understand, do not sign it until the lawyer has explained it to your

---

[6] Even without a written agreement, a valid retainer agreement can be created by oral agreement of the parties or by their conduct. For example, if a lawyer performs services for a person at that person's request or with that person's knowledge, an attorney-client relationship is formed, and the lawyer is entitled to a reasonable fee for the work.

satisfaction. If there are parts of the agreement that you do not like, point these out to the lawyer and ask if they can be changed. If the lawyer will not change the terms you don't like, you will have to decide whether to put up with them or to search for a lawyer whose retainer agreement is more to your liking.

Paying Attorneys' Fees

Lawyers are required by the rules of professional conduct to charge "reasonable" legal fees. Of course, what is reasonable will depend on many factors including the difficulty of the issues presented by each case and the experience and skills of the lawyer. The fees charged by divorce lawyers vary widely, ranging from around $75 an hour up into the hundreds of dollars per hour. Shop around.

Most divorce lawyers charge by the hour. One reason for doing this is that it is almost impossible to predict how much time it will take to handle any divorce case. If the case is very simple, some lawyers will agree to charge a flat rate (some even advertise flat rates for simple cases in the newspaper). Flat rates are the exception, however, and most divorce clients are charged for each hour that the lawyer works on the case, plus any other expenses that the lawyer and client agree will be charged separately. Lawyers in South Carolina are not allowed to use contingency fees in divorce cases. A contingency fee is when a lawyer agrees to represent you for a percentage of what you recover. This is a common practice in personal injury lawsuits, but it is not permitted in divorce cases.

Divorce lawyers charge for every minute they spend on their cases, including brief telephone conversations with clients. For segments of hours, some lawyers only charge for the exact number of minutes they actually work while others round up to the nearest 6, 10, or even 15 minutes. For example, you could have a three minute phone conversation with two lawyers who charge $120 per hour, yet one might bill you $6 and the other might bill you $30 for the same phone conversation. This could become a significant amount of money over the course of your divorce, therefore, you should ask each lawyer how he or she charges for portions of hours worked. If another lawyer in the firm or members of the lawyer's staff such as paralegals will be working on your case, the lawyer should also explain if their time will be billed to you and at what rates.

In addition to attorneys' fees, clients are typically expected to pay other costs such as court filing fees, depositions, private investigators, photographs, psychological evaluations, guardians *ad litem* for children, appraisals, CPA's, and tax consultants. You should ask the lawyer to predict which of these costs the lawyer thinks will be necessary to incur in handling your case and to give you at least a rough estimate of how much you will have to spend on them. Sometimes, clients and lawyers can work together to find ways to reduce or avoid some of the costs.

Some lawyers do not have set rates. Instead, they charge different rates depending on the expected difficulty of the case and other factors. If you contact a lawyer's office that has this practice, it may be worth your time to meet with the lawyer to learn what the lawyer will charge to handle your case, unless the lawyer charges a high fee for the initial meeting.

Most people are more interested in knowing how much the total bill is going to be than what hourly rate the lawyer is charging. You should ask for an estimate of the total charges, including fees and any other costs that will be charged to you. It is very difficult to predict how many hours it will take to handle a divorce from start to finish. A wide variety of factors determine how much time it will take a lawyer to help someone through a divorce and many of the factors simply cannot be evaluated accurately when you and your lawyer are initially agreeing to work together. The most difficult thing for a lawyer to predict is how you and your spouse are going to act throughout the litigation. The cost of a divorce is largely determined by how many issues the parties decide to fight over. Although most issues in divorce cases are settled out of court, no one can predict at the beginning of a case how much trouble it will be to work out a settlement, or even if one is possible. Human behavior is difficult to predict and clients' attitudes and goals sometimes change frequently during the divorce process. An experienced lawyer, however, should be able to make an educated guess about the overall costs, and you should ask for one before deciding to hire a lawyer. Remember, though, that this will be an estimate, not a guarantee.

Most divorce lawyers will ask for a substantial portion of their fees to be paid in advance. These advanced funds are called a "retainer fee." The money will be held in the lawyer's client escrow account, and the lawyer will transfer money from the escrow account to the lawyer's account as the money is earned by the lawyer. If the money in the escrow account runs out or becomes low, the lawyer will ask for more money. Any money that is still in the escrow account that has not been earned by the lawyer must be returned to the client when the attorney-client relationship ends. Lawyers are required to keep very accurate records about escrow accounts.

If you have any questions about how your money is being spent, your lawyer should be willing to provide you with the details. (Many divorce lawyers routinely report to their clients the details of the work they are doing for them and how their money is being spent.)

Most retainer fees in divorce cases are called "special retainers" because they are requested for a specific matter, the divorce. Some divorce lawyers ask potential clients for nonrefundable retainers. If a lawyer asks you for one, request an explanation of its purpose and the circumstances under which it will or will not be refunded. If the intent of the lawyer is that the money will be nonrefundable under any circumstances, irrespective of whether any professional services are actually rendered, you may want to consider hiring a different lawyer. It is not clear whether divorce lawyers in South Carolina are permitted to request nonrefundable retainers in divorce cases under the rules of professional conduct. The South Carolina Supreme Court ruled in a 1999 case that a lawyer committed misconduct by refusing to refund any portion of a purportedly nonrefundable retainer. The Court noted that any fee must be reasonable under the factors outlined in the rules of professional conduct and that any unearned portion must be returned to the client. The Supreme Court specifically declined to decide in that case whether special nonrefundable retainers are legitimate in South Carolina, but it clearly discouraged their use.

Seeking to Have Your Spouse Pay Your Fees and Costs

It is possible for the Family Court to order one spouse to pay the other spouse's attorneys' fees and costs. If you are unable to pay your own attorneys' fees and your spouse has adequate assets, you can ask the Family Court to order your spouse to pay the fees and expenses of your divorce. This must be requested in the pleadings. The Family Court can make the award at the final hearing or it can order temporary payment for work performed prior to the filing of marital litigation as well as the amount of projected fees and expenses needed to prepare the case for trial. It will be up to your lawyer to document his or her fees and costs and to justify them to the Family Court.

The possibility that a Family Court might be persuaded to make your spouse pay for your divorce does not relieve you from your personal obligation to pay your lawyer. Most lawyers are reluctant to represent someone in a divorce on the possibility that the opposing spouse will be ordered to pay their fees. In the first place, there is no guarantee that a Family Court judge will order the other side to pay or that the order will require the other side to pay the total amount of the fees and costs. More often than not, such orders only require the other spouse to pay a portion of the fees and costs. The other problem is that the earliest you can ask a judge to make your spouse pay your fees is at a temporary hearing after the divorce complaint has been filed. Sometimes, the Family Court will not decide whether to award fees and costs until the final divorce hearing. Therefore, your lawyer will expect to be paid by you even if there is a chance that the payments will eventually be reimbursed by your spouse.

The American legal system's practice of imposing a duty on one spouse to pay the other spouse's attorney fees in marital litigation is based on the spouses' mutual duty to provide necessary support for each other. The prevailing view is that when a needy spouse becomes involved in marital litigation, legal services are as necessary an element of support as food and lodging.

Whether to award attorneys' fees is left to the discretion of the trial judge. A fee award must be based upon a reasonable hourly fee. The judge will consider a range of factors in determining whether to award attorneys' fees, but two of the essential factors are a party's ability to pay and the beneficial results obtained. The beneficial results factor means that the Court will not award attorneys' fees, or at least not all of them, if it appears that the lawyer for the requesting party needlessly pursued issues that resulted in no benefit to the client or otherwise wasted the Court's time or that of the other side. This also means that if you unreasonably complicate the case by asking your attorney to raise issues that you do not really intend to pursue (such as child custody), you may end up footing part of the bill for your spouse's attorney.

Even if the Court determines that both parties can afford to pay for their own attorneys, it may still award attorneys' fees to one spouse if it concludes that the other spouse was uncooperative and prolonged and hampered a final resolution of the case.

Attorneys' fees may be awarded on the basis of a party's misconduct irrespective of any other factors, if the party requesting fees is required to incur attorneys' fees due to uncooperative, unreasonable, and contumacious[7] conduct that disrupts, prolongs, or hampers the resolution of issues in marital litigation. Therefore, you should not make false claims nor should you make it more difficult than necessary for the case to go forward.

The Family Court has fairly broad authorization to award litigation expenses as well as attorneys' fees. The same considerations that apply to awarding attorneys' fees also apply to awarding litigation expenses. Reimbursable expenses include the reasonable and necessary expenses incurred in conducting the litigation. For example, travel expenses may be claimed when a parent must travel a distance to protect visitation or custody rights. Expert witness fees may also be recoverable; and if adultery is alleged but denied, a private investigator's fee can be awarded if evidence of adultery is uncovered by the investigator.

The Respective Roles and Expectations of Lawyers and Clients

The relationship between a lawyer and a client in a divorce case should be characterized by teamwork. The details of how the team is organized and who has which responsibilities will not be exactly the same in any two cases, but the lawyer and the client should clearly understand their respective roles and responsibilities. You should try to assist with the work as much as possible. Anything you can do for yourself instead of asking the lawyer or the lawyer's staff to do it will save you money. For example, you may be able to gather and organize documents, to arrange for appraisals, or to ask school teachers or others for statements or records. The more organized you are with records and documents, the less you will be paying someone else to do that organizing for you.

---

[7] Stubbornly refusing to comply with court orders.

The client establishes the specific and overall goals to be accomplished during the divorce process. The lawyer is required to abide by a client's decisions concerning the objectives of representation. The lawyer's role in setting goals is to help the client understand what can be achieved realistically through the litigation process or other means. The lawyer should ensure that the client considers all options that might achieve the client's objectives and that the client understands the possible legal consequences and probable results of each option. A lawyer cannot settle any issue in the case without the client's approval, and a lawyer is required to tell the client about any settlement proposals offered by the other side, good or bad.

The manner in which a client's goals will be achieved is generally left to the lawyer's discretion, but the lawyer is required to consult with the client about the means by which the client's objectives will be pursued. Whenever possible, lawyers should choose more efficient approaches over more expensive ways of getting things done. They should also consult with their clients before committing large amounts of money or time to projects that are not absolutely necessary to protect their clients' interests.

What You Should Expect from Your Lawyer

A client is at a disadvantage in evaluating the quality of legal services. Law practice involves the use of specialized knowledge and skills that nonlawyers do not possess. Therefore, a client cannot effectively evaluate whether he or she is receiving competent legal representation. When a law case ends, a client knows if the results were satisfactory, but a client seldom knows whether a better result was possible or whether any shortcomings were caused by the lawyer's incompetence or negligence.

Divorce clients can, on the other hand, evaluate whether they are receiving client-centered legal representation. The most common reason that clients give when they are dissatisfied with legal services is not that their lawyers charged too much or did not obtain the results they wanted. Rather, the number one complaint of clients who are unhappy with their lawyers is that their lawyers did not seem to care about them or their cases. Some competent lawyers conduct their law practices in a client-centered way, others do not. Lawyers who conduct their business in a way that makes their clients feel cared for will have happier clients than those who don't.

Clients can find lawyers whose practices are client-centered and avoid or fire those whose practices are not. It is not very difficult to identify the signs. Lawyers who practice in a client-centered manner will:

- ▸ treat you with respect and courtesy.

- ▸ be open and honest with you at all times, even if it involves bad news.

- ▸ advise you of the emotional and economic effects of divorce and the possibility or advisability of reconciliation.

- ▸ educate you about the law and the legal and emotional processes of divorces and help you anticipate issues that might arise and fashion responses to them.

- ▸ provide guidance as to how you should conduct yourself in matters such as dating or other socializing, dealing with child visitation, and handling jointly owned property.

- ▸ share decision-making responsibilities with you. A lawyer should provide sufficient information to permit you to make informed decisions regarding the representation including a realistic evaluation of the chances of achieving your goals. This should include counseling you with respect to the law and other considerations such as moral, economic, social, and political factors that might be relevant to your situation. A lawyer should respect your decisions on the objectives to be pursued in your case, including whether or not to settle any issue in your case, and should consult with you as to the means by which your objectives are to be achieved.

► be available when needed.

► demonstrate a willingness to communicate with you and to keep open lines of communication.

► listen to what you have to say and try to understand your viewpoint.

► follow through on promises to you.

► handle each task as promptly and efficiently as possible.

► keep you informed of developments in the case and promptly respond to letters and telephone calls.

► not permit your relatives, friends, employers, or other third persons to interfere with the representation, affect the attorney's independent professional judgment, or make decisions affecting the representation, except with your express consent.

You should have realistic expectations of your lawyer, however, and recognize the limits of a lawyer's role in helping you get through the divorce. Lawyers are counselors in law, but most are not therapists or marriage counselors.

In addition to practicing in a client-centered manner, a lawyer should handle your divorce competently and diligently in accordance with the highest standards of the profession. For example, a divorce lawyer should:

► comply with the rules of professional conduct and other rules of court and with the laws of the United States and

South Carolina. A dishonest act by a lawyer, such as fraud, theft, deceit, or any other conduct that reflects poorly on the lawyer's "fitness" to practice law can result in the loss of the lawyer's license to practice law. Lawyers owe a duty of loyalty and commitment to their clients, but they also owe duties to the legal profession and society in general.

▶ discourage you from engaging in fraud, dishonesty, or criminal conduct. If you persist in such conduct, the lawyer should withdraw from representing you.

▶ encourage the settlement of any contested issues or other marital disputes through negotiation, mediation, or non-binding arbitration.

▶ strive to lower the emotional level in matrimonial disputes and refuse to assist in vindictive conduct toward a spouse or third person.

▶ treat the opposing party and counsel with respect.

▶ not criticize the Court, opposing counsel, or the judicial system unless it is necessary to help you make informed decisions.

▶ not use the discovery process for delay or harassment, for example, by filing frivolous motions or pleadings, submitting burdensome interrogatories, or engaging in obstructionist tactics.

▶ not contest custody or visitation of the children for financial leverage or spite.

▶ consider the welfare of any children affected by the representation. Your lawyer should discourage you from saying anything negative about your spouse to the children and should encourage you to try to foster a good relationship between the children and both parents.

► stick to business. If you and your lawyer decide that you want to pursue a personal romantic relationship, the lawyer should first withdraw from representing you and help you find another lawyer. Divorce lawyers are strictly prohibited from having sexual relations with their clients or opposing counsel during the period of representation.

If your lawyer initiates unwanted sexual advances, you should find another lawyer to handle your divorce and report the forward lawyer to the South Carolina Supreme Court's Commission on Lawyer Conduct by writing to The Commission on Lawyer Conduct, 1220 Senate Street, Suite 305, Columbia, South Carolina 29201. Include as much detail as possible about what happened including copies of any documents that might support your complaint. Be sure to include your name and address as well as that of the lawyer.

If you become unhappy with some aspect of your lawyer's performance, you should promptly inform the lawyer and explain specifically what changes you desire. If your request is reasonable, your lawyer will probably do what you want. If your lawyer does not think that your request is reasonable, listen carefully to your lawyer's response and take time to consider both sides. Even if you are not satisfied with the lawyer's response, resist making a rash decision to change lawyers. First, evaluate whether the problem is affecting the ultimate achievement of your goals and objectives or is simply irritating.

What Your Lawyer Expects from You

Divorce lawyers generally enjoy practicing law. They like to help clients make it through this difficult period of their lives. They usually respect their clients and enjoy their company. However, some clients are easier to enjoy representing than others, and divorce lawyers fear discovering that they have agreed to represent the "client from hell." You should try not to be a difficult client.

One characteristic of difficult clients is intense anger that blinds good judgment. Clients whose decisions are controlled by their hostility toward their spouses make it hard for lawyers to provide effective representation and protect the clients' long term interests. Conversely, clients whose guilt about their divorces makes them want to yield everything to their spouses are almost certain to complain later that their lawyers let them give away too much.

Dishonest clients or those who disobey lawyers' instructions also make their lawyers' lives unduly difficult. For example, a client who tries to hide assets from the other spouse is not helping the lawyer obtain the best possible property division. Clients who saturate their lawyers' phone message centers with trivial issues or expect instantaneous results are not behaving reasonably. You should always consider whether your request is reasonable from the lawyer's perspective.

Divorce lawyers have certain expectations of their clients. You and your lawyer should spend some time discussing these to be sure that you understand them and that you agree they are appropriate expectations that you will try to meet.

All lawyers expect their clients to tell them in clear, specific terms what they want to achieve in the case. Clients who do not express what they want have no right to complain when they don't get it. Do not assume that your lawyer knows your positions about issues in the divorce or understands your fundamental personal values and how they might affect how you want the lawyer to approach the case. At the same time, your lawyer will want you to be realistic in your expectations about the outcome of the divorce and what your lawyer can do for you. Lawyers understand that things sometime change during the divorce process, including clients' priorities and objectives. If yours change, let your lawyer know as soon as possible.

Lawyers also expect clients not to keep secrets from them. Keeping secrets from your lawyer gives power to the other side. You should tell your lawyer everything, including any embarrassing facts or information that you think might hurt your case. You know what you did and your spouse probably does too. If your spouse knows, then your spouse is telling his or her lawyer. You do not want your lawyer to be surprised by harmful information during negotiations or trial. Your lawyer cannot anticipate potential problems or help you decide how best to deal with them if you keep relevant information to yourself.

Above all, do not lie to your lawyer. If the lawyer organizes the case around facts that are false, deceitful, or misleading, the case will fall apart when the other side produces evidence of the truth. Relying on untruthful information would also cause the lawyer to breach his duties as a member of the legal profession, and it could injure the lawyer's reputation and future career.

Lawyers expect clients to ask questions, particularly if clients do not understand something about the information or advice the lawyers are giving them. Lawyers sometimes use words and phrases inadvertently that only other lawyers would understand. They are happy to explain, but sometimes need to be reminded when they are speaking "lawyertalk."

Do not go behind your lawyer's back to get a second opinion about some issue in your case. If you want a second opinion, tell your lawyer that you want to get one before you get it. Ask the second lawyer to communicate directly with your lawyer to ensure that they are both operating on the same information. If your friends and relatives offer advice or information that seems different from your lawyer's, you should tell your lawyer and ask for a clarification.

Keep your lawyer informed of any changes in your life or any events that might be related to the divorce. Unlike many other types of law cases, the relevant facts in divorce cases continue to evolve throughout the process. It may be a good idea to keep a detailed diary in which you record any meetings or conversations with your spouse and any events involving your children.

Your lawyer also expects you to use common sense and discretion in your personal life while the divorce is proceeding. Things that you do after separating from your spouse can affect the results in divorce cases. You should conduct yourself as though everything you do is being observed and recorded and will be reported to the judge at the final court hearing. You should follow the Golden Rule even if your spouse does not.

Lawyers want their clients to let them know if they become unhappy with something about the lawyer or members of the lawyer's staff. Most lawyers want to do good work and to have happy clients. If you are unhappy with the services you are receiving for any reason, you should tell your lawyer.

You should treat your lawyer's staff with courtesy and respect, if you expect the same from them. Make an extra effort to get along with the staff because they will be working on your case, too, and a happy, supportive team is a productive team.

Do not be a pest. It is quite reasonable to expect your lawyer or someone from your lawyer's office to return your phone calls and to communicate regularly with you. It is not reasonable to expect every phone call to be returned immediately. Unless you have a real emergency, don't call your lawyer at home or on the weekend. Divorce lawyers need a break from their jobs just like everyone else, probably more than most. If your husband is a day late with the child support payment, it is not an emergency.

Although your lawyer probably likes you personally, this does not mean that your lawyer is your personal friend. Nor is your lawyer a therapist. If you need one, your lawyer can refer you to one. Divorce will bring changes to your life that will cause you to face many decisions. Some of these will involve legal issues, but more of them will involve social, financial, and other personal matters about which your lawyer has no special expertise. You should not get annoyed with your lawyer for not wanting to spend time advising you about nonlegal matters.

Ending the Lawyer-Client Relationship

Client Fires Lawyer

The client has an absolute right to fire the lawyer at any time for any reason, or for no reason at all. Some people end up with lawyers they don't like, either because they hired the lawyer under time pressures or were not careful about hiring the lawyer for some other reason. Or because they simply made a mistake. If this happens to you, you may want to find a new lawyer. Before you start looking for a new lawyer, however, you should consider giving your present lawyer a chance to fix the problem. Lawyers want their clients to be satisfied with their services, and most lawyers will try to resolve problems that are making their clients unhappy.

Unless there is a compelling reason to do otherwise, you should hire a new attorney before firing the old one, so you won't be left without a lawyer for any period during the divorce process. If you do so, the new attorney should be willing to contact the other attorney to work out transferring the case. (Be aware that some lawyers will not talk to you while you are still represented by someone else. You may have to discharge your lawyer first.)

If you decide to fire your lawyer, the lawyer is entitled to any fees earned up to that point. The lawyer should promptly refund any unearned retainer fees that you paid in advance. If you think the lawyer should not charge you for all the work he has done, ask him to reduce the fee. If he does not and you want to dispute the fee, refer to the section on fee disputes elsewhere in this chapter.

The lawyer should promptly give you or your new attorney your complete file, including any work product created by the attorney (you paid for it). The file belongs to the client, not the lawyer. South Carolina still recognizes a rule of the English common law that gives a lawyer a retaining lien on a client's documents, money, or other property that come into the hands of a lawyer professionally, until a general balance due him for professional services is paid. However, an attorney can only rely on this rule to refuse to turn over a client's file if the client is financially able to pay but deliberately refuses to pay a fee that was clearly agreed upon and is due.

The lawyer bears the burden of proving that the client is deliberately refusing to pay a fee that is clearly due. In addition, the lawyer must establish that the imposition of the lien would not prejudice important rights of the client or other parties and that there are not any less stringent means to resolve the dispute. Some cases and scholars suggest that there are no circumstances under which a retaining lien can be imposed validly, and in fact no modern case in South Carolina has concluded that a lawyer properly asserted a retaining lien. As one of the leading experts on the rules of professional conduct in South Carolina wrote in a 1998 article, "good lawyers understand that retaining liens are for the birds."

Your lawyer should not charge a "closing fee" for closing the file, nor should the lawyer charge you for copying the file (if the lawyer wants to copy portions of the file for the lawyer's records, those copies are for the lawyer's benefit not the client's, and the lawyer should bear the cost of making those copies). If the lawyer claims that fees or other charges for closing a file are called for in the retainer agreement you signed, you should ask another lawyer for an opinion about the validity of such provisions.

If you believe that your lawyer is improperly retaining your file or other property or is charging improper fees for closing your case, you should report this conduct and seek assistance from the South Carolina Supreme Court's Commission on Lawyer Conduct by writing to The Commission on Lawyer Conduct, 1220 Senate Street, Suite 305, Columbia, South Carolina 29201. Include as much detail as possible about what happened including copies of any documents that might support your complaint. Be sure to include your name and address as well as that of the lawyer. You cannot report lawyer misconduct online or over the telephone.

More information can be obtained from the South Carolina Judicial Department website at www.judicial.state.sc.us/discCounsel/howToFile.cfm or www.judicial.state.sc.us/discCounsel/LawyerConductPublicMemberApplication.pdf.

Lawyer Withdraws

Lawyers seldom withdraw once they agree to represent someone in a divorce. There are some occasions, however, in which a lawyer is permitted or even required by the rules of professional conduct to withdraw from representation. For example, a lawyer is *required* to withdraw from representing a client if the representation would cause the lawyer to violate a law or the rules of professional conduct (for example, due to a conflict of interest), or if the lawyer's physical or mental condition materially impairs the lawyer's ability to represent the client.

Some of the circumstances under which a lawyer is *permitted*, but not required, to withdraw include when a client persists in a course of action involving the lawyer's services that the lawyer believes is criminal or fraudulent, when the client insists on pursuing an objective that the lawyer considers repugnant or imprudent, if the client fails substantially to fulfill an obligation to the lawyer (for example, paying for the lawyer's services), or where the representation would result in an unreasonable financial burden on the lawyer or has been rendered unreasonably difficult by the client.

Once a lawyer makes a formal appearance and becomes the attorney of record in a divorce or other court action (by filing pleadings, for example), the lawyer cannot withdraw without permission of a Family Court judge. Permission is routinely granted if another lawyer notifies the Court that he or she is representing the client and will be the new lawyer of record.

In withdrawing from representation, a lawyer should always do so in a manner that will not have a material adverse effect on the interests of the client. A withdrawing lawyer should give reasonable notice to the client and give the client time to hire another lawyer. The lawyer should also surrender any papers and property to which the client is entitled and should refund any fees that were paid in advance but not earned.

Case Ends

When the case is over, the attorney-client relationship ends unless the contract between the lawyer and client provides otherwise. A case involving litigation is "over" when the final order is filed and served. A case that does not involve litigation ends whenever the lawyer finishes providing whatever legal services the client requested. If your case involves litigation that results in a court order, the lawyer should provide you with a copy of the final order that shows on the front page when it was clocked in (filed) by the office of the Clerk of the Family Court (the clocked in date on the order is the official date of your divorce). The lawyer should also return to you any original documents of yours that are in the file as well as anything else in the file that you would like to have.

The lawyer should give you a final accounting of all fees and costs, and he should return any unearned retainer fees that you paid in advance.

If everything did not turn out exactly like you hoped or expected it would, the lawyer should explain why this happened and should discuss with you the possible outcomes of an appeal and how much one would cost (unless motions to reconsider or other post-trial motions are filed). A notice of either party's intention to appeal must be filed within 30 days after receiving the divorce decree.

Another important topic to discuss with the lawyer is what you should do if any problems related to the divorce arise in the future, for example, alimony payments, property division, child visitation. You may specifically want to discuss what role the lawyer is willing or would like to play if such problems arise.

Fee Disputes

You have a right to expect your lawyer to provide you with competent legal services for a reasonable price. Even when there is a fee agreement between the attorney and the client, the rules of professional conduct mandate that the fee must be reasonable. High fees are not necessarily unreasonable. The fees and costs of getting divorced can become quite significant in some cases when the lawyer has to work a large number of hours to pursue the results desired by the client. It is the lawyer's responsibility to keep you informed about the expected and actual costs of handling your divorce. You should not be caught by surprise when the final accounting is made.

Your lawyer expects you to pay the reasonable costs of handling your divorce. If a lawyer does not get paid, she cannot operate her office or support her family. If she did not expect you to pay her, she would have chosen to help other people with their divorces, not you. If you have a legitimate fee dispute with the lawyer, raise it and get it resolved. Otherwise, you should pay your lawyer what you agreed to pay when you hired her.

If you believe that your lawyer's fee is unreasonable, you have several options. The first thing you should do is to tell your lawyer that you think the lawyer is charging you too much or is charging you for unnecessary work. Despite the reputation of the legal profession, most divorce lawyers want their clients to feel that they are getting their money's worth. They want their clients to be as happy as possible with their services and the fees they charge. They want their present and former clients to refer future clients to them. Most fee disputes are resolved quickly and to the clients' satisfaction. Don't be afraid to let your lawyer know if you become unhappy about some aspect of the fees you are being charged. Lawyers cannot fix problems they do not know about.

If you are not satisfied with your lawyer's response to your concerns about fees, the best option may be to ask the Resolution of Fee Disputes Board of the South Carolina Bar to help resolve the matter. Of course, you could simply refuse to pay (and risk being sued by your lawyer) or you could bring a lawsuit to recover previous payments for charges that you thought were unreasonably high. Most people, however, would prefer to avoid the costs, stress, and time required for litigation, and the Resolution of Fee Disputes Board offers an option to clients of South Carolina lawyers that is not available in all other states.

The Resolution of Fee Disputes Board exists solely to provide an alternative to litigation when lawyers and clients, or lawyers and lawyers, are unable to resolve disagreements about fees. The amount of the fee in dispute must be less than $50,000. No fee dispute may be filed with the Board more than three years after the dispute arises. The dispute cannot be pending in a court. All proceedings are confidential. The services of the Board are free.

The fee dispute resolution process is initiated when either a lawyer or a client files a written complaint explaining the circumstances surrounding the dispute with the South Carolina Bar, P.O. Box 608, Columbia, SC 29202-0608 (803-799-6653). Forms and information about the fee disputes process are located in the Public Information section of the Bar's website, www.scbar.org.

Once a complaint is filed, the Board has exclusive jurisdiction to render a final decision. A client cannot be forced to submit to the jurisdiction of the Board. However, once a client consents in writing to the Board's jurisdiction, the client will be bound by its final decision. If a client files a complaint with the Board, a lawyer must submit to its jurisdiction and will be bound by the final decision of the Board.

The first thing that will happen is that a member of the Board will be assigned to encourage an amicable, voluntary resolution of the dispute, perhaps through mediation.[8] If the parties settle the dispute, the chairperson will send a letter confirming the agreement. This agreement becomes binding 15 days from the date of the chairperson's confirmation letter.

If the parties cannot reach an agreement, the assigned Board member will investigate the dispute and submit written recommendations to the chair of the Board for the judicial circuit

---

[8] If the amount in dispute if more than $7,500, the chairperson of the Board for the judicial circuit where the parties live (circuit chairperson) is allowed to appoint a hearing panel instead of assigning the matter to a member of the Board.

where the parties live. These recommendations will be submitted within 90 days and all fee disputes should be resolved within six months, although extensions for good cause may be granted. If the chairperson concurs with the assigned member's recommendations and the amount in controversy is less than $7,500, this is the final decision of the Board.

If the chairperson does not concur with the recommendations of the investigating member, a hearing panel will be appointed consisting of three members of the Board. At the hearing before the panel, the parties can represent themselves or they can be represented by counsel of their choosing. The Board is permitted to appoint a lawyer to represent a client who is not represented by one already, but only for good cause (considerations of income level, education, or in the interests of justice).

The panel will conduct a hearing and make an entirely new investigation of the fee dispute. The panel members will not receive the investigating member's report or the circuit chairperson's final decision.

The matter may be withdrawn from the jurisdiction of the Board by consent of all parties. Lawyers are not allowed to withdraw unless the client consents. If a client withdraws from the proceedings, the withdrawal will end the proceeding with prejudice and the client will not be allowed to file a subsequent complaint with the Board about the same dispute. The Board will remind the client of the preclusive effect of withdrawal, and if the initiating party does not make a written acknowledgment of the withdrawal the panel will proceed to decide the matter.

Once a decision is reached, it can be enforced in any court of competent jurisdiction. Compliance with the panel's decision should take place within 30 days after the mailing of the decision. The decision of the panel is final and binding. It can be appealed to the Circuit Court within 30 days.

Malpractice or Other Unprofessional Conduct

Most lawyers in South Carolina are honest and competent. Unfortunately, a few bad lawyers can spoil the reputations of all lawyers. If you believe your lawyer has engaged in dishonest or fraudulent conduct or has somehow harmed you through negligent or intentional acts, you should not ignore it. If you learn upon investigating the matter that you were mistaken, you will feel better about your lawyer and avoid the possibility that you might unfairly damage the lawyer's reputation and livelihood. If on the other hand you learn that your concerns are well-founded, you will provide a valuable service to the public and to the legal profession by exposing the lawyer's misconduct.

There are two options you may want to consider for initially investigating your suspicions. The preferred option should be to discuss your concerns with your lawyer if you feel comfortable doing that. There are frequently very good explanations for conduct that may seem questionable. If you do not feel comfortable talking to your lawyer about the problem, consider asking a second lawyer for an opinion and for guidance about what to do.

If your suspicions appear to have merit, you can report the misconduct to the South Carolina Supreme Court's Commission on Lawyer Conduct by writing to The Commission on Lawyer Conduct, 1220 Senate Street, Suite 305, Columbia, South Carolina 29201. Include as much detail as possible about what happened including copies of any documents that might support your complaint. Be sure to include your name and address as well as that of the lawyer. You cannot report lawyer misconduct online or over the telephone.

More information can be obtained from the South Carolina Judicial Department website at www.judicial.state.sc.us/discCounsel/howToFile.cfm or www.judicial.state.sc.us/discCounsel/LawyerConductPublicMemberApplication.pdf.

You should not complain to the Commission on Lawyer Conduct about trivial matters that do not reflect on a lawyer's fitness to practice law. Some of the types of misconduct that may subject a lawyer to professional disciplinary action include: committing a criminal act; engaging in conduct involving moral turpitude; engaging in conduct involving dishonesty, fraud, deceit or misrepresentation; stating or implying an ability to influence improperly a government agency or official; and having sexual relations with a client.

If you were harmed by the lawyer's misconduct and the lawyer is unwilling to compensate you, you may have no option other than to file a lawsuit for malpractice. If this is an option you might consider, you should seek legal advice and assistance without delay. Any action for malpractice must be commenced within three years after you knew, or by the exercise of reasonable diligence should have known, that your lawyer may have committed malpractice.

Another option may be to apply for compensation from the Lawyers' Fund for Client Protection of the South Carolina Bar. The purpose of the fund is to compensate clients who suffer certain types of losses because of lawyers' dishonest conduct. A client can seek reimbursement within three years of the date the client discovered or should have discovered the dishonest conduct but never later than six years from the date of the dishonest conduct. The maximum reimbursement from the Fund is $20,000. Also, the Fund will only reimburse a client in circumstances where the client cannot recover the loss from the lawyer, for example, if the lawyer has been disbarred or suspended from the practice of law, has died, has disappeared, has removed himself from the State and is not subject to judicial process, has been declared by a court to be bankrupt, or has been declared by a court to be mentally incompetent. To apply for reimbursement, a client should obtain a "Form of Application for Reimbursement" from the South Carolina Bar, P.O. Box 608, Columbia, SC 29202-0608 (803-799-6653) and mail it to the Lawyers' Fund for Client Protection of the South Carolina Bar at the same address. If the claim appears to have merit, the Lawyers' Fund For Client Protection Committee will conduct an investigation and determine how much money, if any, will be paid to the client from the Fund.

Marriage and Divorce Law in South Carolina

INDEX

Paternity, establishing, 153—156

Registry of Foreign Support, 164

Remarriage, 176

Retroactive, 152

Seizure of property, 169

Shared parenting adjustment, 162

Tax consequences, 162—163

Unemployment insurance benefits and, 171

Visitation and, 147

Child Support Enforcement, South Carolina Division of, 154—155, 163, 169, 175

Child Support Guidelines, South Carolina, 31, 67, 154—155, 159—162, 187

Child Support Recovery Act, federal, 171

Children

Care, 18

Criminal sexual conduct and minor, 96

Disability, physical or mental, 157—158

Divorce and, 23—24, 27—28, 64

Domestic violence, 89

Education, 18

Legitimacy, 17—18

Names of, 18

Welfare, 18

Circuit court, 222

Cohabitation

Alimony, 175

Annulment and, 40

Gifts, 111

Going business, valuation of, 114—115

Grandparents, visitation, 149—150

Guardian *ad litem*, 78, 132—136, 142, 202

Haiti, 45

Harassment, 101—109

Health, physical and emotional, 116

Health and Environmental Control (DHEC), South Carolina
Department of, 7

Hearing

    Final, 66, 80—83

    Notice of, 79

    Pendente lite, 73

    Temporary, 73—75

Homosexual

    Child custody, 141

    Divorce, 50

Hotlines, 97—98

Identification, 111—114

Illegitimate child, 17—18, 128, 152

Incest, 10, 40

Income of spouses, 116

Income tax refund, withholding, 170

Individual Retirement Account (IRA), 113

Inheritance, 16—17

Initial meeting with attorney, 196—199

Internal Revenue Service (IRS), United States, 127, 170—171

Interstate custody disputes, 143—145

Intestacy, 16

Joint assets, maintaining reasonable access to, 32—33

Joint custody, 130—131, 137—138

Judicial Department, South Carolina, 217, 223

Justice, United States Department of, 101

Lawyer

Agreements with spouse regarding divorce, 29

Alimony, 174

Appeals, 84—85

Closing fee, 216—217

Confidentiality, 197

Consulting with, 173

Custody, 178

Escrow account, 203

Family court, representation in, 65

Fee disputes, 219—223

Fees, payment of, 201—206

Files, 216

Final order, 82

Financial Declaration form, 72

Guardian *ad litem*, 134—136

Hearing, 80—83

Hiring, 192—196

Initial meeting, 196—199

Malpractice, 197, 223—225

Need for, determining, 187—190

Notice of appeal, 84

Retirement benefits, 113, 117

Retirement plan, 115

Separate maintenance, 117

Social Security benefits, 113

State disability retirement benefits, 114

Support obligations, prior marriage, 117

Tax consequences, 117, 119

Training, need for additional, 116

Transmutation, 112

Valuation, 114—115

Protection from Domestic Abuse statute, South Carolina, 26, 99

Provocation, defense of, 61—62

Psychological evaluation, 202

Psychological parent, 142, 151

Reasonable attorney's fees, 201

Reconciliation, 48, 54, 61, 80

Recrimination, defense of, 59

Refund of attorney's fees, 204, 216

Registry of Foreign Support, 164

Rehabilitative alimony, 124

Reimbursement alimony, 124

Remarriage

Generally, 185—186

Child custody, 177

Child support, 176

Removing child from state, 128—129

Residency requirement for divorce, 45—46

Resolution of Fee Disputes Board, South Carolina Bar, 220—222